JUSTICE
GONE
WRONG

A SHERIFF'S POWER OF FEAR

Isaac M. Flores

iUniverse, Inc.
New York   Bloomington

Justice Gone Wrong
A Sheriff's Power of Fear

iUniverse books may be ordered through booksellers or by contacting:

iUniverse
1663 Liberty Drive
Bloomington, IN 47403
www.iuniverse.com
1-800-Authors (1-800-288-4677)

Because of the dynamic nature of the Internet, any Web addresses or links contained in this book may have changed since publication and may no longer be valid. The views expressed in this work are solely those of the author and do not necessarily reflect the views of the publisher, and the publisher hereby disclaims any responsibility for them.

ISBN: 978-1-4401-2828-8 (pbk)
ISBN: 978-1-4401-2829-5 (ebk)

Printed in the United States of America

iUniverse rev. date: 3/30/09

This book is affectionately dedicated to my family
— Michael, Cathy, Alexa and Alissa
— and to my late wife, Dorothy Ann Chambers Flores

Contents

Photographs

CHAPTER 1

DEATH ROW PICKUP

The grimfaced sheriff drove his brand-new Olds 98 sedan right up to the side entrance of Florida State Prison to pick up two death row inmates. He was transporting the convicts back to his Lake County jail for a new trial.

Willis McCall, tall and big-boned, sported well-shined cowboy boots. Along with a gray suit and white shirt, he wore a black string tie and white cowboy hat. His gold badge gleamed in the lights, and a pearl-handled pistol was strapped to his waist under his jacket. He arrived at the prison alone, in the dark, despite his strong view that these were two dangerous criminals who ought to stay right there and get what they deserved – the electric chair.

The two convicts, Samuel Shepherd and Walter Irvin, were weighed down by heavy leg shackles as they shuffled into the brightly lit prison lobby under guard. Their heads were down, looking at their feet as they tried to shield their eyes from the unaccustomed glare, made even harsher by the white tiles.

"A lot of people in Lake County would like to get ahold of these young fellers and string 'em up from a tree right now. They raped a white woman," Sheriff McCall repeated the inmates' history to prison officials.

The prison, known simply as Raiford, is part of a complex consisting of three institutions near the small community of Starke, tucked away in the North Florida backwoods.

The sheriff was taking precautions because there *had* been a lynching attempt back home when the two men were arrested two years earlier. How and when he was transporting the prisoners back to Lake County for a new trial was his well-kept secret. Only McCall and a trusted deputy knew about the midnight transfer.

The officers briskly chained the inmates' handcuffs to each other and manhandled them out the door and into the sheriff's big car. They were thrust onto the passenger side of the bench-like seat.

"Hitch 'em good," the sheriff told the guards who brought them out to his car. "I don't want 'em making any moves against me on the road." Both men would be riding up front with him "so that I don't get any surprises," he explained while moving his pistol to his left hip.

The sheriff quickly signed the papers transferring the two frightened, wild-eyed convicts to his custody. The prison people were not, of course, unaware of the highly controversial nature of the case and the volatility of white people in Central Florida's Lake County, which backed onto the wilderness area that would later become the sprawling Walt Disney World tourist complex.

What was left unsaid and didn't need explanation was that this was a time when segregation was still the practice, if not the law, in many parts of the South, including much of Florida.

In Lake County, as in many Southern areas, blacks still lived in the poorest sections of town, still sat in the back of the bus, still had to use separate public toilets and water fountains. They couldn't legally sit down at a restaurant or attend "white" schools. In general terms, they were tolerated as long as they had didn't make a big fuss.

Everyone knew the sheriff as a tough guy when it came to Negroes, as the blacks were generally known. They were often nigras, niggers or coloreds to McCall and the people of Lake County.

"Nigras are all right so long as they know their own place and stay there," McCall would repeat over and over to anyone who would listen. "When you get a handful of 'em together, you're gonna have a little bolita, a little moonshine and a whole lot of sex. Anybody that doesn't know that doesn't understand them."

The rape of a white woman by blacks was not merely a grievous sin to these church-going merchants, farmers, growers and citrus industry workers. It was something to be quickly avenged with summary punishment for the culprits, if possible. That was a strong-held belief in this part of the state, along with other Southern areas — something that shocked many outsiders.

Now, in carrying out the court-ordered return of the prisoners from Florida's death house to the county jail, Sheriff McCall would have only the assistance of his most-trusted deputy, James Yates. The deputy, who was also the sheriff's close friend, would be traveling in a lead car and was to function as scout and escort to spot any possible trouble along the one-hundred mile route on the less-traveled roads between Raiford and the jail.

The lockup was on the second floor of the old courthouse building in the Lake County seat of Tavares.

Much against the sheriff's desires, a cranky old judge back home was following a higher mandate in ordering that the two men be retried. The United States Supreme Court had been called on to rule in the rape case, and the court had immediately handed down a ruling resounding throughout the South.

Everyone but McCall, it seems, had expected the high court's intervention in the controversial, highly publicized trial outcome.

Reports of jailhouse beatings for confessions and other maltreatment by the sheriff and his men had prompted separate investigations by state and federal officials. Two special grand juries found no civil rights violations during the arrest and incarceration of the black defendants, however.

They were tried together, convicted and sentenced to death by an all-white jury.

Attorneys for Shepherd and Irvin carried their appeals through the Florida legal system and eventually to the U.S. Supreme Court. And when it received the case, the nation's highest tribunal was appalled by what had transpired in Lake County.

The justices voted unanimously to order a new trial.

The blistering opinion by the Supreme Court reversed the trial court verdict and appellate ruling by the Florida Supreme Court that had kept the men on death row. The Supreme Court of the United States decried the fact that the circuit court trial had been carried out in "an incendiary atmosphere." It declared that the case had "stirred deep racial feelings . . . exploited to the limit by the press."

Actually, three young black men had gone on trial on the rape and kidnapping charges. All were convicted. Shepherd and Irvin were given the death penalty, but the all-white, all-male jury had been more lenient toward Charles Greenlee, who was only 16 years old. The trial jury recommended a life sentence and that's what the judge imposed.

Lawyers for Greenlee did not contest the verdict and sentence, and his case was separated from the appellate process involving the other two defendants.

A fourth suspect fled before arresting officers could get to him in the hours after the kidnap and rape of the woman.

But the black man was quickly identified, pursued and eventually tracked down in a distant county by a posse of white men on foot and horseback. Reporters were informed that the suspect, Ernest Thomas, was shot and killed by volleys of rifle, shotgun and handgun fire while trying to hide in the Florida scrubland.

"He got what he deserved," said one of the posse's leaders, Ed Rincon.

Now, Sheriff McCall — citing the temper of the times — told friends he would get the two remaining prisoners back to his own jail safely for retrial, but in his own way. This turned out to be in secret and in the middle of the night!

"I'm not taking any chances with them or with any of these hotheads in this county," McCall vowed. "I've had my fill of lawyers and prosecutors and judges and some of the crazy people around here who would rather lynch 'em than try 'em."

The sheriff, of course, was of the school that believed in trying them first and *then* lynching them.

McCall always followed his own ideas of law and order, which he always pronounced as one word: *lawandorder*. That's the only way he thought of it. He also believed that since he was sheriff, there was just one way to interpret it — *his* way.

The sheriff wasn't just talking big. There *had* been big trouble. There had been plenty of mob action and an attempt to bust into the Tavares jail by an angry crowd of white men. There had been riots, and the urgent need to call out the Florida National Guard to restore order in Lake County.

The case turned out to be one of Florida's most notorious, and the state was no slouch along those lines. The Groveland Rape Case had long-lasting repercussions, which no one could have foreseen. The bright spotlight of unsought and unwanted publicity generated by that one criminal act and trial was forever to stain Lake County and Sheriff Willis V. McCall.

The arrest of the three blacks, and the manhunt and killing of the fourth suspect brought international repercussions to a region of Florida which was then largely unknown except for its beautiful, productive citrus groves.

There was no glamorous Walt Disney World in what was then McCall's bailiwick.

CHAPTER 2

RAPE VICTIM

Rosemary Jane Davis was seventeen, thin and pale. She fidgeted with her curled, blonde hair and compressed her thin lips tightly as she took the witness stand in the hot, muggy courtroom to tell the all-male jury about her ordeal.

She told the silent courtroom about attending a dance with her husband, Homer, and how they had been set upon as they experienced car problems on a dark country road by four black men in a passing car.

Rosemary's voice lowered as she explained what happened next.

"One of them said, 'Grab the lady' and two of them got me and forced me to get in their car."

The vehicle then sped off down the main highway between the communities of Central Hill and Okahumpka.

The driver turned off onto an old, abandoned broken-pavement road. Rosemary said she didn't resist because she was scared that they might kill her.

Prosecutor Jesse Hunter gently prodded the witness: "Now, on that drive from where they took you from your husband 'til they got to the place they stopped, tell the jury what happened."

"Well, on the way out there, after they pulled in and backed out from that road, well, this Thomas nigger —later I learned his name — well, he forced me to pull, jerked up, my dress. And I pulled it back down and he jerked it up again, and he told me to leave it alone.

"He was pointing a gun at me. And so he made me pull off my pants, and he still had the gun on me and when we got out to that place and . . ." Her voice trailed off. "Well, he raped me first."

Question — "Did they take anything from you?"

Answer — "Yes sir: my rings and my compact, my powder, perfume . . . and I believe that's all."

Q. — "Did they do anything to you on the road going out there?"

A. — "Only one of them, Irvin, he tried to love on me. After I first got in the car."

Q. — "Tell the jury what they did when they got there."

A. — "Well, after we stopped, they turned off the lights and the Thomas nigger raped me first and while . . ."

Q. — "Go ahead and tell them what happened. Don't tell them that they raped you. What did happen? What did he do to you."

A. — "Well, he shoved me down on the seat and he pulled my legs apart and got on me and he kissed me and then he put his thing into my privates."

Q. — "Did he have intercourse with you?"

A. — "Yes sir."

Q. — "Then what happened?"

A. — "Then the Thomas nigger, he got out and then Irvin, he raped me"

Q. — "The same way?"

A .— No sir. The Thomas nigger, he got out and got in the front and then Irvin, he taken me and done me the same way. Only he didn't kiss me."

Q. — "What happened then, after Irvin and Thomas got through?"

A. — "Well, I don't know which one was the next one that done it."

Q. — "Then what happened?"

A. — "Then one of the others. I don't know which one it was."

Q. — "Did all of them have intercourse with you that way?"

A. — "Yes sir."

Chapter 3

Sheriff Notified

McCall was driving back to Florida from Cleveland with a couple of friends when he first heard about the rape case in his own backyard. He had attended a national Elks Club convention and enjoyed the camaraderie with his friends for several days. Cleveland was all right, he and his friends decided. But now they were anxious to get back to Lake County and attend to their business.

As usual, McCall liked to drive, and he was at the wheel of his own Oldsmobile. He liked a big car, and he had outfitted it with everything he needed as a sheriff when he was on the road.

He and his lifelong friends, Byron Herlong and Frank Stephens, were accompanied by one of the sheriff's deputies, Doug Sewell, who had hitched a ride with his boss in Columbus, Ohio. Also with them was a prisoner Sewell had retrieved from jail officials in Columbus to be returned to Tavares for trial in a break-in and assault case.

Driving through the tiny north-central Florida town of Citra, McCall flicked on the police radio he had installed in the Olds.

"We're probably too far away to get anything from Tavares on this thing," the sheriff told his companions.

But suddenly, amid the squawk and static, McCall heard the

call sign and radio traffic out of his own office. Picking up the microphone, he announced himself to the dispatcher.

The voice of jailer Reuben Hatcher came on, weak but distinct: "Boy, am I glad to hear from you, sheriff. We had a bad rape case last night down in Groveland. A white housewife raped by four Negroes . . . Some of the people down in that area are making all kinds of threats and there's a lot of trouble fixin' to start. We've got three of the suspects in jail."

It was the 95-degree afternoon of Saturday, July 16, 1949.

Sheriff McCall knew the kind of trouble that could start over an incident like this. "Rape by Negroes" was a phrase calculated to inflame the tempers of white men to violence.

The sheriff's jurisdiction squatted in the middle of the state, which had never really been considered part of the "deep South" or its traditions and often-rebellious ways.

Sleepy Lake County, forty miles wide and seventy-plus miles long, was dotted by small towns, many smaller than little Tavares, and crisscrossed by narrow two-lane roads. It was home to around 30,000 people, about one-fourth of them black. The endless, ordered citrus groves, alternately green or golden depending on the season, provided gainful employment for many whites and a greater number of black citizens — men, women and children.

Lake County was citrus wealthy. County affairs were firmly controlled by wealthy growers and town merchants, plus the sheriff and other white elected officials.

The county was aptly named. The sparsely settled area — to the north and west of what is now Walt Disney World — was one of Florida's richest agricultural areas, strewn with picturesque lakes, orange groves and gently rolling hills covered in pine and moss-draped live oak. Its well-groomed little towns had names like Mount Dora, Umatilla, Yalaha and the "triangle" communities of Tavares, Leesburg and Eustis.

Mulling over the possibility of trouble brewing in his domain, the sheriff gunned the car. "Take it easy, Willis," said Herlong, uncomfortable about the sudden jump in speed of the vehicle now barreling down U.S. Highway 301.

"Sorry, boys," McCall drawled. "But I gotta get back quick."

That short radio transmission was, to Sheriff Willis McCall, the start of the Groveland Rape Case.

CHAPTER 4

ARRESTS AND LYNCHING ATTEMPT

Sheriff Willis McCall (just plain "Willis" to his wife and friends) was thirty-nine years old, six-foot-two and two-hundred thirty pounds. He looked more like a young western lawman than today's movie and television stereotype of a paunchy southern sheriff.

His big, meaty hands gripped the car's steering wheel tight. His size twelve feet usually sported high heel boots and he was given to wearing a white Stetson hat and western clothes. He chomped down on a big cigar as he worried about what was going on back home in his absence.

First elected to the job in 1944, McCall had come to it with no experience and little training. But that was not unusual in a state with few standards for election and appointment of sheriffs, legislators, municipal and county officers, even judges.

He got his job by defeating five other men in the Democratic primary. There was no Republican opposition. Hardly ever was.

Now in his second four-year term, his training had been on the job. "Being a good sheriff just takes good judgment," McCall told the voters in 1944. "I have to earn the respect of the citizens." And he had done more than that. He became so popular and well-known throughout the area that he won reelection by a two-to-one margin in 1948.

He stepped into a hornet's nest when he returned to the Tavares jail.

Three young blacks were in the lock-up at the Lake County courthouse building. They were suspected of the rape of the young housewife from the hamlet of Bay Lake, in the southwestern section of the county.

As the couple later testified, they had been out having a good time, dancing and chatting with friends at the American Legion Hall in the nearby town of Clermont. They left when the music ended early Saturday morning. As they were leaving, Davis had trouble with his battered 1940 Ford and needed help in pushing it to get it started.

Once under way, the couple drove west on State Road 50 through Groveland then made a right turn along a dark roadway leading through citrus groves toward an all-night diner in Okahumpka. Along the way, the couple quarreled and Davis decided to turn back. As he stopped to make a U-turn, the car stalled again just off the road.

Four young blacks were driving by. They stopped and offered to help. The men then suddenly turned on Davis, beat him up and left him nearly unconscious alongside the road. They forced the woman into their own car. The assailants drove for some distance, then stopped and parked the car and took turns raping her at gunpoint, Rosemary Davis said.

Afterward, they gave her the option of going with them "and getting killed" or getting out of the vehicle and walking. She chose to walk. Dazed and disheveled she hurried away and hid in the woods as her attackers roared off.

She remained hidden until almost daybreak, and then fearfully walked the six miles to the hamlet of Okahumpka. There, she approached the first person she came to, a night watchman, and asked him to drive her back to the place where the attackers had left her husband.

By this time, Homer Davis had recovered and gotten help with his car. He started driving north to Leesburg to report the kidnapping and was going through Okahumpka when he encountered the vehicle bearing his wife.

A few hours later, Samuel Shepherd and Walter Irvin were arrested because the description of the dark sedan they had been driving tallied with that given by the rape victim.

Charles Greenlee was picked up later that morning for carrying a weapon, and Mrs. Davis tentatively identified the teenager as another of her assailants. The man said to be the fourth attacker, Ernest Thomas, was still at large.

Sheriff McCall hadn't been back at the jail very long that evening when he was told that a motorcade of 20-30 vehicles, carrying armed and angry white men, was on its way from Groveland to the jail in Tavares, a distance of about 20 miles.

"They's probably about 100 of them vigilantes, and they got weapons of every kind," deputy Johnny Josephs reported to McCall. "They's wanting to force their way in here and drag out the rapists and string 'em up."

McCall went into action.

He ordered Deputy Yates to hustle Shepherd and Irvin out of a back door in handcuffs and into a waiting car. He didn't move Greenlee because he knew the lawbreakers didn't know about his arrest. They were after Shepherd and Irvin.

Yates and Eustis Police Chief Bill Olson drove the two prisoners to the sheriff's house in Eustis, less than five miles from the jail.

The sheriff had a big split-level home on a hillside. A big garage ran underneath a part of the house, and the prisoners were taken in there. They sat in that makeshift hideaway under the guns and watchful eyes of Yates and Olson while the half-crazed hotheads descended on the Tavares jail.

Their intention was "to hang their black asses," as one of the ringleaders bluntly proclaimed.

Shepherd and Irvin, both 22 years old, had been in trouble

with the law before and were known to many of the residents of the Groveland-Bay Lake area. Greenlee was not. He was arrested on an unrelated charge, gun possession. And the sheriff was right: most members of the mob outside didn't connect him to the others.

The streets and parking areas around the Lake County courthouse quickly filled up as the sullen, sunburned farmers and townspeople drove up in their dusty cars and pickups that sultry evening. Among them were the victim's husband, Homer Davis, and her father, William.

Muttering and cursing among themselves, some of them carrying weapons openly, a group of the men moved quickly toward the back entrance of the stately old building which housed the jail. Another contingent started going right up the front steps of the building toward the entrance.

Suddenly, out in front, a crowd of reporters and townspeople saw the handsome double doors fly open. Sheriff McCall walked out and down the courthouse steps right into the middle of the crowd. Unarmed and hatless, he greeted some of the angry men by name and asked for quiet.

"I can't let you people do this,'" he began in a loud, firm voice. "We can't allow things like this. You fellas elected me to uphold the law, and I've got to do it. I may be in sympathy, and I know you're stirred up about this thing. You've got a right to be. But you don't have a right to take the law into your own hands."

Besides, the sheriff told the mob in a more conciliatory tone, "The prisoners you want are no longer here. They've been taken elsewhere."

"Look, McCall," shouted one of the group's ringleaders, "We're going to fix them niggers right now or none of our women is gonna be safe."

Others yelled out obscenities and called the sheriff a liar. They threatened to bust into the jail to see for themselves whether Shepherd and Irvin were gone.

After more heated discussion, McCall dealt his card. "All

right," he said, "I'll appoint a small delegation to go inside and look so that you can see that they're gone. But just three of you, that's all. The rest of you stay out here."

The sheriff pointed to the young woman's husband and her father and told them to pick out a third man. Then he escorted them up the courthouse steps and upstairs to the jail.

The other protesters stayed outside. A couple of uniformed deputies stood nervously just inside the double doors in the courthouse lobby. But they made no move for the weapons strapped to their sides.

The inspection tour by the mob's three representatives quickly discovered that Shepherd and Irvin were not in the jail — a grimy, stucco-walled facility where black and white inmates occupied separate areas.

When informed of this finding, the crowd again became belligerent. The frustrated ringleaders demanded to know where the prisoners had been taken. But McCall — by this time sitting on the courthouse steps with several of the most-outspoken members of the noisy group – did some fancy doubletalking.

"Now, I know most of you as sober, reasonable fellas," McCall told them, raising his voice above normal conversation level. The crowd quieted a bit.

"You've got families and responsibilities. I'm sure you have many things to do on a Saturday evening besides sit here and argue with me about some nigras. I've secured them, and that's all there is to it. I've got to follow the law. Now, you fellas give it up and go on about your business. Some of your wives are probably waiting supper, or they may be wantin' for you to take 'em out to a movie or something."

The mob began to break up a bit, but some still hung on, arguing among themselves and shouting out questions at the sheriff until a thundershower came up and many of them went skittering under storefronts. Soon, everything was back to Saturday-evening normal. Individually and in small groups, the men had taken their axe handles, clubs and deer rifles and stowed them back in their cars and pickups and headed on home.

Sheriff McCall was a hero in newspapers across the state and around the country as a result of that encounter.

"Sheriff Outtalks Mob in Tavares Rape Case," Reported the St. Petersburg Times early Sunday morning. "Sheriff Staves Off Lynching," shouted a headline on a paper in Eugene, Oregon.

The rape case and "lynch mob" story was prominently displayed in newspapers in New York, Los Angeles, Dallas and Chicago as well as throughout the Old South. It was on the radio and even on the television.

McCall told reporters that letting three of the angry men walk through the jail "was the easiest way I could think of to quiet them down. I could've stood out there and gotten angry and mean and called out the deputies and barricaded the jail. But I was trying to avoid bloodshed. I was trying to smooth it over and get them to cool off."

As soon as the noisy group of would-be vigilantes departed, the relieved sheriff called the Raiford prison and received permission to send the prisoners there temporarily. Actually, he found out later, he could have transferred them right away instead of hiding them out in his house, where his wife Doris and their youngest child had remained throughout the tense confrontation.

The sullen members of the Groveland-Bay Lake contingent had not been appeased, however. And McCall's problems were far from over, as he soon found out.

CHAPTER 5

MOB MAYHEM AND GUARD PATROLS

Frustrated by the sheriff after working themselves into a lynching fever, many of the rabblerousers didn't go home after they left the Tavares jail.

Those who did and went about their Saturday chores later regrouped with their still-aroused friends and neighbors. They gathered on street corners, in bars and backyards, talking over the day's events, reluctant to let such a revolting thing as the rape of a white woman take place in their midst and not do anything about it.

Negroes were supposed to know their place, to hold jobs, support their families and stay out of trouble. Most of all: *Stay away from white women.*

Late that night, they erupted, reorganizing into a mob that had earlier experienced a taste of power. They mobilized — breaking the stillness of the hot, humid night with the belching roar of cars, pickups and even some lumbering, fruit harvest six-wheelers, all setting out for the shantytowns nearby.

The white troublemakers thundered through the darkened roadways and alleys, firing shotgun blasts into the Blue Moon Café, owned by Ernest Thomas' mother, and breaking out all the windows. The night riders then descended on the Bay Lake community, shooting into a house where the Shepherd family lived, spraying surrounding homesteads. Farther down the road, many of the 400 Negro residents of Groveland were frightened out of their homes and fled into the woods.

Scores of terrorized blacks were driven off to safety in trucks provided by some of the more responsible white citizens.

After several hours of venting their emotions, the armed riders finally dispersed, disappearing from the roads back to their homes and families. The night became still once again.

Sheriff McCall and his deputies, now working with several units of the Florida Highway Patrol and local police officers, had been unable to keep up with all of the fast-moving events that night, however. And at daybreak on Sunday, the exasperated sheriff was forced to call Gov. Fuller Warren and ask that National Guard troops be sent to Groveland and vicinity.

Hearing his story, the governor quickly agreed and ordered 50 armed guardsmen from Leesburg and Eustis to move in as a precautionary measure. The violence was believed to be a one-time flare-up that wouldn't recur. Surprisingly, no one had been hurt. The Negro residents who fled had now returned home.

Everything was quiet this Sunday morning. But it didn't stay that way.

As the Guard troops were still being mobilized, the Ku Klux Klan got into the act.

A long caravan of cars, most of them bearing license plates from neighboring counties, drove slowly through Groveland that afternoon. Their white occupants distributed leaflets, some of them recruitment documents for the KKK while others were plainly designed to incite whites against blacks. Some of the materials, eight-page foldouts, bore the title "Ideals of the Ku Klux Klan." They were printed by The Associated Klans of Georgia.

Another motorcade of some fifteen vehicles drove into Clermont, about six miles east of Groveland, apparently on a similar mission that same afternoon.

"These guys were definitely trying to get the whites to rise up, as they put it, against the Negroes," one white resident of Clermont said. "They said they wanted to help us out in doing that. They didn't say how. . . But they didn't stick around long when they didn't get a good reception. Can you imagine that?"

The overall situation remained relatively normal the rest of Sunday. Most of the Negro residents of Groveland, Mascotte and other communities either stayed quietly out of sight or moved out for the night to stay with friends and relatives who lived farther out.

National Guard troops began arriving early Monday in Tavares, and everyone, white and black, went about his or her business in a relatively normal fashion during the day — pestered only by newspeople, who they mostly ignored.

Trouble broke out again after nightfall.

A mob of about 50 white men invaded the Negro neighborhood of Stuckey's Still, on the western edge of Groveland. The invaders drove through in cars and trucks, firing shotguns, pistols and rifles into the air and into some of the now-abandoned homes. Some 25 families fled from their homes as the loud motorcade approached.

Sheriff McCall was patrolling in his car when the trouble broke out. He was accompanied by a couple of volunteer deputies. A radio report alerted them to the activity at Stuckey's Still, and the sheriff quickly turned his car around and headed in that direction.

"Willis, you better not go down there. They'll kill you. That mob will stop at nothin'," one of the deputies, a storekeeper named Jefferson Clinton, told the sheriff.

"Jeff, I'll stop and let you get out if you want to, but I don't have any choice," McCall replied. He took off his white Stetson and threw it on the back seat of the car. "I've got to go down there."

Special deputy Clinton stayed put, as did the other young man, Rufe Collis.

They could hear the shooting as they approached the piney

woods area in the dark. As soon as the sheriff saw the knot of milling men in his car's headlights, he screeched the vehicle to a stop, jumped out and fired a teargas bomb right into their midst. This got most of them moving toward their own cars and trucks. Others simply ran off into the woods. Those in their vehicles sped off in a single file, made a large U-turn at the far edge of the neighborhood and, driving across U.S. Highway 50, parked one-by-one in the dark woods and turned off their vehicle lights, watching and waiting.

With smoke and gas still spewing from his teargas gun, the agitated sheriff got back into his car and started after those staying behind. But the daring move came to a sudden halt when teargas filled the vehicle, giving McCall, Clinton and young Collis a choking fit before they could clear it and get under way again.

"Sons of bitches. Now they got me mad," said the sheriff as Clinton cowered down in the seat next to McCall and Collis fingered the teargas gun through an open window in the back seat.

Once more, the sheriff drove right into the band of terrorists, most of them now crowding around a couple of the lead trucks. McCall stopped, got out of the car and began trying to talk them into dispersing.

"You fellas don't want to do this," he shouted. "You're breaking the law, and I want you to know I'll arrest you. You got no business here. Go on home."

"We wanna wipe this place clean of niggers," came a retort out of the dark.

The milling men, angered by the teargas, were now cursing the sheriff, arguing with each other and threatening to drive over to nearby Mascotte and Groveland.

"Fellas, you're just going to mess everybody in this whole community up." McCall tried to be heard above the hubbub. "You're going to get a lot of people in trouble and your families are going to suffer for it, and we just can't have it . . . Sit down and think it over; talk it over. Don't go out there and do something you're going to be sorry for."

After a few minutes of this, most of the disgruntled men got back into their vehicles and drove slowly on down the road. But when they got to Mascotte, a village of about three hundred residents, many of the vehicles pulled in and the men again spilled out of their cars and trucks.

They joined an unruly mob already in town taunting a few National Guard troopers, who were nervously patrolling the streets and trying to keep some semblance of order. One man approached a Guardsman whom he knew and yelled in his face: "Why don't you take that peashooter and go home. You look like a Boy Scout."

"I bet it ain't even loaded," another man jeered.

At that, the trooper pointed the weapon to the ground and fired twice, asking the startled onlookers if that sounded like a Boy Scout with a peashooter. But that didn't settle anything.

Some of the agitators, wielding sticks and armed with rifles, lined the main street of the tiny business section, which consisted of several stores, a restaurant, a couple of bars and one outdoor telephone booth.

Emmett Peter Jr., an investigative reporter for the *Tampa Tribune*, later wrote, "Many of those in the crowd were in cattle trucks, poking their guns and rifles through the slotted sides right at the National Guardsmen. They had at least three cattle trucks that I saw, right in the middle of town. They had every Guardsman covered. The Guard was clearly outnumbered and outgunned."

Also to be glimpsed in the melee were Negroes and some of the white residents running into the woods and side streets.

The sheriff, who had kept right on the tail of the first group, quickly jumped out of his car, stalked over into the middle of the crowd and once again tried to placate the hotheads. But to little avail.

While angry talk and threats swirled about on the dimly lit

streets, a reporter from Atlanta sidled up to harried McCall and demanded that the sheriff give him names.

"Names? What names?" the angry sheriff replied, wiping his brow with a broad handkerchief.

"Who are those firebrands over there?" the reporter shouted and pointed. "Give us the names of those men leading all these troublemakers. The ones you earlier put the tear gas on. You're going to arrest them, aren't you?" persisted the newspaperman.

"I don't know the names. I don't know who they are," shouted back the exasperated sheriff.

The brief exchange was overheard by a balding, beefy roughneck.

"You hear what the sheriff told that goddamn reporter?" the sputtering, red-faced fellow asked those around him. "I'm gonna go straighten the little bastard out. I'll give him names . . ." The belligerent man made his way over to where McCall was standing. Yelling and waving his arms to get attention above the noise, he bellowed: "Where's that goddamn son of a bitch wanted my name? I'll tell him my goddamn name and I'll fix his ass, too."

The sheriff slowly looked around, spotted the short, balding newspaperman a few paces away taking in the action. But McCall turned back to the tough guy, shrugged his shoulders and said, "I don't know where he went. He was standing right here a minute ago."

Several newspeople were directly threatened by the loudmouths and told to get out of town, accusing them of writing and broadcasting lies about what was taking place in Lake County.

All this time, McCall had been trying to talk the loudest of the rabblerousers into calling it a night before someone got hurt or the National Guard was forced to intervene aggressively. The situation did, at last, start to calm down when, suddenly, another contingent of Guard troops drove onto the scene.

The troops jumped down from their vehicles and began ordering the crowds off the street.

This brought tempers to a boil again. Shouts and curses

echoed in the still air. Some members of the mob took to taunt-ing the newly arrived Lake County Guard members, uniformed and carrying carbines.

"What the hell are them bastards doing here now?" demand-ed one of the loudmouths, marching right up to stand nose-to-nose with the sheriff.

"Ralph, I asked for them to try to calm everything down. Now just go over there and tell your fellas to go on home or there are going to be some arrests."

"By God, we ain't standing for this." the stout farmer shouted back over his shoulder as he moved away. "We may just start shootin' here and now."

At this, Sheriff McCall turned on his heel and bulled his way through the crowd up to the Guard unit's commander, Lieuten-ant Jim Hershey. Nearby reporters clearly heard this exchange: "Jim, how about you just take some of your men and go down the road a little bit. Just move them away from the middle here, and if I need you, I'll call you right back quick. . . Maybe if you get out of sight, they'll go on."

Reluctantly, the Guard officer agreed, and his unit moved off. The pullback relieved the tension and the explosive atmosphere enveloping the hamlet of Mascotte this sweltering night.

The big cattle trucks carrying armed terrorists began backing up and moving out. Other vehicles started dispersing, the men moving out individually and in small groups as if suddenly de-ciding they'd had enough adventure for one night.

Soon, McCall and several of his men stood alone, talking quietly among themselves in the middle of the street. Reporters now created the only noise, a chatter that soon turned into a lot of running-about and shouts competing for attention from the sheriff, the Guard commander and storekeepers who hadn't fled the town.

The one public phone booth was lit up and swallowing dimes and quarters fast as reporters called in their stories.

"Why didn't you arrest some of those guys?" was a question

asked repeatedly of the sheriff. "Are you going to make a list of names and turn it into the governor?" "What are you going to say to Governor Warren?" "How come nobody's been put in jail except those Negroes?"

Some early radio and newspaper reports the following day were critical about how the episode was handled.

"Just like a couple of generals on the battlefield," one article scoffed about the conference between the sheriff and the Guard commander.

But this night hadn't ended. Lake County continued to smolder in the wake of the rape case.

CHAPTER 6

"HERO" SHERIFF QUELLS VIOLENCE

While McCall and his small number of deputies, along with Hershey's unit of Guardsmen, were dealing with the situation in Mascotte, another, smaller group of whites was up to mischief in Groveland. They filled the air with gunshots, scaring away residents in the black neighborhood. They set fire to several houses.

Among the properties destroyed was that of Henry Shepherd, an uncle of one of the rape suspects.

Two of the houses damaged were owned by George Valree, a Negro fortune teller. Shortly after the marauders first began appearing in town, the frightened Valree ran to a local merchant, L. Day Edge, and asked him whether he thought Valree should get out of town. "Well, I don't know," Edge replied. "Maybe you should look into your crystal ball."

Valree didn't stick around and do that.

The sheriff and National Guard officers saw the smoke and flames from Mascotte, but by the time they got to Groveland, only the burning houses were in evidence.

The sheriff, the Guard and a few Highway Patrol troopers set up a temporary command post at Groveland High School. At one point, a Guard officer got on the telephone with Governor Warren and recommended the immediate arrest of some of the known mob ringleaders. Overhearing this exchange, McCall grabbed the telephone and bluntly told the governor that, in his opinion, to arrest anyone at that point "will be like lighting a match under a powder keg. If you want to do that, I want you to relieve me of my responsibility here."

The governor agreed that the sheriff was in charge, and it seemed to him as if he was proceeding in the right way. The sheriff slammed down the field phone and announced to those present that no arrests were to be made.

But, not much later, the sheriff called the governor and requested that more National Guard troops be sent.

By Tuesday, there were more than 200 Guardsmen patrolling that area of once-peaceful Lake County. Another 100 arrived that night, armed with carbines and pistols.

Meanwhile, McCall and State Attorney Jesse Hunter, who together knew just about everybody in the country, made the rounds and prevailed upon merchants and professional people to use their influence in their communities to help them squelch the rioting. Among those intervening in this way was Edge, who owned a large mercantile store and other businesses that virtually constituted the whole downtown section of Groveland.

"Our main concern was that four or five men that was hot-headed as hell was stirring things up," McCall said. "It didn't take much to stir-up right then because, you know, it was a hot issue. If they could've got those nigras out of that jail, they would have lynched them; they would have."

Whether it was the sheriff's actions or the heavy presence of the Guard, racist anger had run its course, the mob violence was over in Lake County. Everyone expected wholesale arrests – or at least of some of the ringleaders. But no arrests were made.

McCall loudly defended his actions.

"Nobody got hurt," the sheriff kept repeating. "Nobody got a scratch, and that's what I was trying to keep from happening. White or black, nobody got hurt. If I had arrested one man, there would have been bloodshed. There was no way we could have kept from it. I'm not going to apologize to anybody for the way I handled that thing."

While McCall was criticized by some, others agreed with his handling of the situation.

The *Miami Herald* said in an editorial: "When the mob spirit dies down, when sober judgment returns to Lake County, the people of that terror-beleaguered community will congratulate themselves on the character of the sheriff they had during the nights of gunplay, arson and threatening demands that the Negroes be turned over" to the mob.

The editorial went on to say that the sheriff had stood firmly and wouldn't be swayed by mob anger. "He was the law. Thanks to his steadfast courage, Florida has been saved from the blackening disgrace of a lynching."

The *Sarasota Herald-Tribune* was another newspaper with high praise. It declared that if McCall had shown the same attitude that "too many Southern sheriffs have shown in the past, Florida would have received a blot on its record that would have taken years to erase. . ."

Mabel Reese, the co-owner with her husband Paul of the weekly *Topic* newspaper in Mount Dora, praised the sheriff highly for his stand in turning back the armed mobs. "He put to use, objectively, his understanding of the problems of the backwoods people of Lake County," she wrote.

A postcard signed only "a St. Louisan" and addressed to "Sheriff, Groveland, Fla.," said, "You are a REAL sheriff."

Friends and strangers sent McCall clips out of the *New York Times*, the *Chicago Tribune*, the Los Angeles papers and others. Longtime supporters and those who voted him into office — citrus growers, businesspeople, farmers, other county residents — showered him with praise.

In short, Sheriff Willis V. McCall was a hero, the toast of the country.

He didn't have long to enjoy that feeling, however.

CHAPTER 7

ORIGINS AND FIVE-POINT STAR

McCall had enjoyed considerable success since his election as sheriff in 1944.

He was a big, outgoing man who had grown up among the people who had twice named him to the office. Ultra-conservative, dogged in his beliefs, he had a slow, quiet way of delivering his very definite opinions. His political support originated in the citrus industry with owners and growers, and the managers of the citrus cooperatives that sorted, packed and shipped the fruit that wasn't sold for processing. McCall had been a part of the industry as a young man.

After his election as sheriff, he developed into a canny, instinctive politician often going out of his way with a big smile to befriend young and old, newcomers as well as members of the established families of Lake County.

He had been raised on a ranch. And as a backwoods fellow himself, he also had a natural way of relating to people, black and white, who lived simple lives away from the well-traveled highways.

He slowly built a reputation as an aggressive lawman, fearless and outspoken in his defense of law and order, that phrase always spoken by him as if it were one sacred word: *lawandorder*.

Although he often said his only guide as sheriff was maintaining that control, neither he nor the rest of the leadership of little Lake County was greatly influenced — one way or another — by the law of the land concerning black people. He and other county leaders ignored current federal statutes, constitutional rulings and doctrines about school integration, and about housing, jobs, welfare.

But, then, they were not alone in this, either in Florida or any of the surrounding states. In this respect, this part of Florida was truly part of the Deep South. In effect, Lake County reflected many of the South's socio-economic values and practiced its own harsh brand of law enforcement *vis. a vis.* the Negro population.

To most Southerners of this period (including many Floridians), the imposition of outside ideas was to be resisted at all costs. For them, the separation of the races was the natural, accepted way. No Civil War or man-made laws could change that.

McCall believed, as did many other southerners, that Negroes and whites could exist peaceably alongside each other so long as the Negroes knew their "place" in that society. McCall liked some black people as individuals, but over the years he had come to expect a certain respect and deference from them. He was the law, and he interpreted and practiced his own brand of it.

His imposing authority figure was intimidating to many of the younger blacks. They called him "the Big Hat Man" because the white Stetson was the first thing they saw as he came toward them from a distance or drove by in his car.

If he had to muscle them around now and then to remind them of their station in life, that was just the way things were.

One of the first things he did after his election was to begin vigorously enforcing an anti-vagrancy law. He would jail every youth in the county who wasn't working or in the Army. Most of those who wound up behind bars were young blacks, so his reputation as a racist was born. He later defended this by saying anyone who wasn't working (meaning the citrus groves) was "disrespecting the reputation of our armed forces and our boys who faced the bullets and gave up their lives in the war."

As for federal laws, he once told me, "I think the races should work and live and deal with each other . . . But I don't think they should be forced to mingle. I don't think a social life should be forced on anyone, white or black."

Those were McCall's beliefs. Many of his neighbors felt exactly the same way. They had elected him and supported him and expected him to defend those principles. This was not viewed as prejudice. It was the maintenance of the status quo, the earlier, simpler days before outsiders and the federal government started demanding changes.

Iconic Sheriff — He was known by black people in Central Florida's Lake County as "The Big Hat Man." His big, white Stetson was the first thing they saw coming down the road. (photo courtesy of Leesburg Commercial – Leesburg, Fla).

CHAPTER 8

MANHUNT AND DEATH

After the weekend violence, and with Shepherd, Irvin and Greenlee safely in jail, there was still the fourth suspect to be accounted
for. Now that everything was under control, McCall turned his
attention to the missing man, Ernest Thomas.

Thomas had been identified from photos shown the rape victim. The sheriff and his investigators soon determined that he had
a girlfriend who lived near Gainesville, home of the University
of Florida and almost one hundred miles north of Groveland, a
drive of about three hours in those days.

McCall hurried to Gainesville. Explaining his mission to Ala-
chua County authorities, he and a Gainesville Police Department
officer drove immediately to the girlfriend's house. She told them
she hadn't seen or heard from Thomas for weeks.

They suspected her of lying.

McCall went back there the following day. He explained to
me what happened next.

Nosing around, he soon discovered a letter in the young
woman's mailbox. Ignoring postal regulations, he took the letter addressed to her and steamed it open. It was from a Willie
Green and gave a postal route and box number in the town of

Shady Grove, another hundred miles to the northwest and about twenty-five miles from the Georgia border.

After resealing and replacing the letter, McCall alerted the sheriff in Taylor County, in which Shady Grove was situated. Later, they discovered that the postal address was in a neighboring county, Madison, in a community known as Moseley Hall. Authorities there were quickly notified.

The lawmen and volunteers, including some from Lake County, formed a raiding party.

About 3 o'clock in the morning, they descended on the neighborhood, figuring that everyone would be asleep and they would have less trouble. But, somehow, they went to the wrong house, the one next door to where "Green," or Thomas, was hiding out.

While the officers were trying to roust the sleeping people inside the first house, Thomas jumped out a back window in the house next door and took off. The officers called for reinforcements, and an oldtime posse was formed and was soon chasing after the wanted man through the woods and swampland of North Florida.

One of the specially trained dogs, a non-vicious tracker, soon became impatient of the restraint imposed by his master's long leash and broke loose. All day long the search party of about forty men, on foot and on horseback, followed the marks left by the dog's heavy leather leash as the hound tracked Thomas.

Suddenly, toward evening, the fugitive was spotted running across an open field. He ignored shouts to halt and give himself up while a half dozen men on horseback chased him as far as they could into the woods, firing their pistols and rifles. But — much like the posses chasing after the bank robbers in Western films — they missed their target. The desperate Thomas reached the safety of a swamp and got away.

All that night and into the following day, the trackers tracked the dog tracking the fugitive.

At mid-morning, the posse of tired men came upon its

quarry. Bone-weary from the long, exhausting escape attempt, Thomas was asleep under a tree with the tracking dog curled up beside him. Heedless of the notoriety of his prey, the dog was also getting some badly needed shuteye. He had done his job, the hound must have figured. He had tracked him down; now it was time to rest.

Hearing the noise being made by his pursuers, Thomas roused and jumped up, a pistol in hand. The men in the posse's vanguard opened up on him with their shotguns, pistols and deer rifles.

Witnesses at an inquest held in a neighboring town concluded that at least six members of the search party had fired and hit Thomas when he raised up pointing the gun. An autopsy showed that the body was riddled with buckshot, .38-caliber slugs from police weapons and bullets from other types of firearms.

McCall, one of three sheriffs riding at the tail end of the posse, was not in on the fatal shooting. He arrived on the scene minutes later, drawn by the intense gunfire.

"With all that shooting, it's a wonder they didn't kill the dog, too," he said laconically.

Buckshot went through one of the dog's ears and the skin of a leg, but he wasn't badly hurt. "That was some tracker," the sheriff said.

McCall brought back to Groveland one of the shells of a .38-caliber slug pumped into Thomas. He presented it to the rape victim.

CHAPTER 9

TRIAL PRELIMS

Some two-hundred National Guard troops were still patrolling in Groveland, Mascotte and Tavares when Circuit Judge Truman G. Futch impaneled a grand jury, which promptly proceeded to indict Shepherd, Irvin and Greenlee. There was only one black man on the grand jury.

Sheriff McCall announced to one and all that he had obtained confessions from the three defendants and that the statements would be introduced at the trial. "They are the guilty parties. They will get the electric chair," the sheriff proclaimed.

The NAACP, civil rights leaders and a few public supporters of the three men claimed that the suspects had been beaten and tortured during their incarceration. They pointed out that the sheriff and his men failed to investigate the case fully and that the victim's identification of her attackers was faulty. There were grave doubts among them and members of the legal profession that the black men could get a fair trial in Lake County.

Some of the calmer citizens questioned why there had been no arrests and charges brought against any of the rioters, even long after the tension had died down.

But the sheriff answered to no one about any of this.

There was no Miranda rule, guaranteeing prisoners' rights, at the time. Much depended on the whim of arresting officers and court officials. But to be black and suspected of a crime, particularly in rural areas, was downright dangerous for any suspect.

In common with most southern lawmen of the time, McCall was convinced that much of the crime and civil disturbance were committed by the lower classes, especially Negroes. "White trash" often fared no better at the hands of overzealous men charged with enforcement of the law. Their brand of justice was usually quick and often merciless.

The terrorism unleashed by the mobs of white men in Lake County was soon followed by detailed newspaper accounts, interviews, opinions and editorials, many of them directly or indirectly inciting racism. A newspaper in an adjacent county published a large cartoon on its front page showing four electric chairs. Its large caption read, "NO COMPROMISE ——SUPREME PENALTY."

"We'll wait on the law now," one of the vigilantes told a reporter. "But if it don't do the right thing, we will."

The *Pittsburgh Courier*, which circulated among many blacks throughout the country, rushed reporters to Lake County and published several Florida editions during this period. One account from Groveland described "a sordid tale of inhuman bestiality and brutality." The story was under a front-page headline reading: 3 SUSPECTS TIED TO PIPES, BEATEN.

"Brutality in prison" was uncovered by investigators from the National Association for the Advancement of Colored People (NAACP), which quoted the three prisoners as saying that arresting officers had "plied horsewhips to their bodies" to get them to confess to rape.

In response to the emotions and the controversy raised by the case, the NAACP dispatched its special counsel, Franklin Williams, to Florida to work with a local attorney. But it took more than a month before any local trial lawyer would even consider the case.

Alex Akerman Jr., of nearby Orlando, finally agreed to represent the defendants. He did so, he told me in a later interview, because the court-appointed defense counsel refused to seek a change of venue or a delay in the trial.

Akerman, an ex-legislator and the son of a former federal judge, was a Republican when it wasn't quite respectable to be a Republican in Florida. Political labels meant pretty much the opposite of what they do today — Florida Democrats were deeply conservative, Republicans more liberal. Akerman was graying, smooth and businesslike, even eloquent in a quiet way. He was politically ambitious and some said he believed he could make a big name for himself if he could adequately defend three Negroes in a county full of redneck racists.

And that's exactly what he would have to do since quirky Judge Futch refused a change of venue.

Presiding at a pretrial hearing, the judge noted that Williams, the NAACP's lawyer, had been on the case since July 31 and had repeatedly stated that he was sure of the defendants' innocence. That being the case, the judge reasoned, the NAACP counsel must have had time for "a thorough investigation of all the proceedings."

Futch was a colorful former legislator and self-taught lawyer who presided over a trial while whittling on a piece of wood with his pocketknife. Square-jawed and big-jowled, he had been president of the Florida Senate in the 1930s, as a Democrat.

Like most of his fellow Lake Countians, he was politically conservative, and he resented the very idea that outsiders such as those from the NAACP and their liberal, white lawyer from the big city of Orlando could come into his courtroom and make demands.

The prevailing feeling in Lake County was expressed in the catch phrase, "outside agitators." They were all sticking their noses where they didn't belong.

The NAACP's Williams — an aggressive, sometimes abrasive lawyer — and the defendants contended prior to the hearing that the jailed men had been severely beaten with rubber hoses and kicked by deputies after their arrest. Sheriff McCall publicly denied the allegations.

During the three-day pretrial hearing, Irvin attempted to testify that he had been mistreated. Judge Futch abruptly cut him off and ruled the testimony irrelevant.

State Attorney Hunter, a shrewd, veteran prosecutor, brought to the stand several businessmen who testified there was no prejudice against Negroes in Lake County.

The witnesses told how some 400 Negroes had been evacuated by responsible white citizens concerned for their safety after the angry mob tried to break into the jail to lynch the defendants and then terrorized the Groveland area for three nights.

One state witness called the violence "an orderly sort of disorder."

Finally, Judge Futch put aside his whittling, banged his gavel and brought the pretrial peoceedings to a halt. Ruling against the motions for a change of venue and a postponement, he said, "Enough time has been spent on motions to prepare this or any other case."

The trial began on the first day of September, a little more than six weeks after the crime was committed. Speedy justice was the order of the day.

Out of a list of 300 potential jurors, three were Negroes. Only one was called, and he was rejected outright. So it was an all-white male jury that heard the case in the county courthouse in Tavares.

CHAPTER 10

ALL-WHITE JURY FOR GROVELAND TRIAL

The trial was a big production for those willing to overcome the heat and overcrowded conditions. The sweaty spectators included some 50 blacks in a small section in the courtroom balcony and several hundred whites packed into the hard pew-like benches down below. A waist-high railing separated the spectators from the judge's bench, the lawyers' tables, the witness stand and jury box.

Overhead fans did nothing but stir the humid air.

Hunter wanted a quick trial. While the verdict appeared almost a foregone conclusion, he worried about the presence of the outside lawyers and the widespread publicity the case generated.

In his late 60s nearing the end of almost three decades as a prosecutor, Hunter was an unpretentious, plainspoken country lawyer. A popular homespun raconteur, he was used to having his way in Lake County both politically and in court, where he was thorough and meticulous. His round spectacles and mild manner were deceptive: He was one of the best trial lawyers in the state.

Testimony brought out that the Davises were married when Rosemary Jane was 16 and separated before she was 17. She was living with her parents at the time she accompanied her estranged husband to the Clermont Legion Hall to attend the square dance on July 15.

Homer Davis, close to 30, lived with his mother.

He had consumed a bottle of whiskey he purchased prior to their arrival at the dance hall. Both he and his teenage wife told the same story about the car troubles after leaving the dance, getting the car started, about having a quarrel and getting the car stalled again off the Groveland-Okahumpka road.

After the Negroes drove up and started helping out, they abruptly stopped while pushing the vehicle back onto the road from where Davis had backed onto the dirt shoulder. The suspects began whispering among themselves, Davis told the jury. He became suspicious and confronted them with a stick he found by the road. He said he argued with them for a few minutes and then became angry and started swinging the stick at the four men.

They overpowered him, beat him and threw him into bushes across the road and drove off with Mrs. Davis in their own car, according to his testimony.

Initially, Rosemary was shy and awkward over the retelling of her ordeal. But her blue eyes sparked as she gained confidence in telling her story.

Hunter wanted the jury to hear every tidbit, however, and he guided and prodded Mrs. Davis into testifying about the small details. "What is it that he actually did? That was a frequent question to the slim, prim woman.

After the car drove off, leaving her husband behind, Thomas pointed a gun at her and ordered her to remove her underpants, Rosemary Davis testified. Thomas fondled her, and then raped her after the car stopped on an abandoned, dead-end road, she whispered to the court. Thomas then exchanged places with Irvin in the back seat, and he raped her too, she said.

The other two followed Irvin, the young woman testified.

After that, they ordered her out of the car and drove off.

She walked about six miles, hiding in the woods and staying off the main road until she came to Okahumpka, where she found a night watchman who listened to her story and drove her back to the scene to look for her husband. Davis and a friend had been out searching for her, and they hurriedly took her to the Groveland jail at the city hall.

"Why did they do that?" inquired the prosecutor.

"They (officers) told me they had one in there and would I go in and identify him," Mrs. Davis replied. ". . . and I told them I didn't want to and that I was dirty. And they told me to go ahead. And so I went in there where the cells was at and identified him, and I come back out."

That turned out to be the tall, lanky, 16-year-old Greenlee. He was being held for illegal gun possession. In fact, trial testimony later showed he was holding the gun that Thomas had given him hours before.

Her husband and sheriff's deputies told Rosemary at that point that they had an automobile they wanted her to see. She examined the car, a 1940s Mercury sedan, and identified it as the one she had been in.

A few days after the incident, the state attorney himself drove her to Raiford prison, where Shepherd and Irvin were pointed out to her. For the first time, she identified them as two of her attackers. Greenlee also was at Raiford at that point. The three were being held there while awaiting trial.

It was again a packed courtroom on the second day of the trial — an unusual Saturday session. Akerman brought the three defendants to the witness stand after Hunter has paraded all his witnesses through. Dressed in dungarees and T-shirts, they took turns denying under questioning that they were even in the area where the woman was raped.

The defense contended that the Davises were mistaken about the attackers' identities and that the real rapists were still on the loose.

Franklin Williams, The NAACP lawyer, who assisted Akerman, later told reporters that the defense believed the prosecution had manufactured its evidence with the help of McCall and his deputies. But Akerman and Williams presented no evidence of this.

Walter Irvin, a short, husky youth with muscular arms, and the taller, grim-looking Sam Shepherd told the jury they had made the rounds of bars in Lake County and Orlando neighborhoods together that night, drinking beer during the time they supposedly committed the crime. Greenlee and Thomas were not with them, each replied under Akerman's questioning.

In his nervous, rambling testimony, Shepherd did admit to a confrontation at one of the bars with Ernest Thomas that night over a woman they both had dated. But that was the extent of a defense effort to show Thomas and Shepherd were not friendly and were not together throughout the night.

Irvin said he and Shepherd had returned to Lake County sometime before dawn and went home and went to bed. Shepherd testified similarly. Thomas was dead and had nobody to defend him.

The teenaged Greenlee, who had spent much of the first day of the trial playing with a rubber band, drew laughter with his drawl and colloquial expressions. He testified he had been with Thomas, but not with Shepherd and Irvin.

Shepherd and Irvin had been awakened and arrested at their homes the morning of the crime. Greenlee was picked up later.

The mother of Thomas, the fugitive killed by the posse, was brought to the stand by the prosecutor and over Akerman's objections reluctantly testified that her son told her on July 15th – the night of the crime – that he was going out "for a good time" with Shepherd and Irvin. This naturally buttressed the prosecution's case that Thomas had been with all the defendants that night.

The prosecution also presented moldings of tire tracks taken by Deputy James Yates at the scene of the Davises' assault. Yates said they matched those of the car driven by Shepherd. Castings were also made of Irvin's footprints at the crime scene, the deputy said.

The defense attorney contended in his closing argument that the identifications of the defendants made by the Davises were faulty and inconsistent. The time factor placed all three young men elsewhere, not at the crime scene, and the prisoners were beaten to get "confessions," Akerman argued. Mrs. Thomas' testimony about her son was pure hearsay, and should not have been permitted. The defense could not challenge the testimony of a dead person!

The jury deliberated about two hours after dinner before announcing it had a verdict. It was close to 9 p.m. The judge warned the spectators that there should be no demonstration by any of the several hundred spectators, which this day included about 70 blacks in the balcony. The 12 men on the jury filed in and sat down. Jury foreman Charles Blaze delivered the verdict.

All three defendants were found guilty.

The judge agreed to delay sentencing for three days so that the defense could prepare its appeal. He then he exited with a flourish, his black robes sending some of his wood shavings flying.

To a hushed courtroom of black and white onlookers, Hunter declared: "This is the verdict of the people of Lake County. I ask you to accept it and to retire quietly to your homes."

Most of them did.

Three days later, Futch listened to Akerman plead for a new trial by citing a long list of errors he said the judge and the prosecutor had committed in the course of the proceedings.

The whittlin' judge did not take this quietly. He accused the defense of injecting "racial politics" into the case, disagreed with its conclusions and ruled against the motion for a new trial.

Futch then ordered that Shepherd and Irvin be put to death in the electric chair. Because the jury recommended mercy for the teenager, the judge sentenced Greenlee, to life in prison.

CHAPTER 11

PROTESTS, JURIES, STATE AND FEDERAL PROBES

There were vociferous protests by the NAACP and other organizations and some newspapers, particularly from outside the state, that the defendants had been railroaded. Defense attorney Akerman synthesized most of the criticism in his appeal to the Florida Supreme Court. He said:

— A fair trial had been impossible in Lake County because of the prejudice incited against the defendants.

— The defense had not been granted enough time to prepare its case.

— The defendants had not been tried by a jury of their peers because Negroes had been kept off the jury.

— The defendants had been deprived of their constitutional rights because they were beaten by sheriff's deputies after their arrest.

— The state had failed to prove its case against them.

While Akerman had praised McCall for "preventing the lynching of Shepherd and Irvin," he now said the sheriff "wanted to maintain *his* type of law and order and that was it. There was no other."

About six weeks after the trial, a "Committee of 100," a nationwide organization of influential citizens, stepped into the arena with a fundraising appeal for $20,000 "to fight this case through the U.S. Supreme Court."

Among the listed members of the group were actress Tallulah Bankhead, writer Van Wyck Brooks, Socialist Party leader Norman Thomas, psychiatrist Karl Menninger, United Nations Rep. Ralph J. Bunche and novelist Dorothy Canfield Fisher.

The group mailed letters, advertised its case in newspapers and contacted other prominent people throughout the country in a plea for money, calling the sentences "a tragic perversion of justice."

"A careful study of the evidence and the facts in the case proves the absolute impossibility of Greenlee's guilt and the almost certain innocence of Walter Irvin and Samuel Shepherd," it contended. "These young men have been condemned to death not because they are guilty but simply because they are black."

A federal grand jury was convened the following April in Ocala, in neighboring Marion County, to determine if the prisoners had had their civil rights violated in what came to known as the Groveland Rape Case. The jury was to look particularly into the reports of beatings.

Presenting the case to the grand jury was Tampa-based U.S. Attorney Herbert S. Phillips. The investigation was conducted by the FBI.

The Justice Department investigation and grand jury were the direct result of pressure from the NAACP, groups such as the Committee of 100, and the widespread media attention to the case since it began. Public opinion soared. There were arguments public and private on both sides.

In Lake County, State Attorney Hunter blamed the investigation on what he called sensationalized accounts of the case in publications in the North, particularly the reports by Ted Poston of the *New York Post Home News* and counsel Franklin Williams of the NAACP.

Poston, a black, attended the Tavares trial for the specialized edition of that newspaper, and his accounts were harshly critical of "Southern Justice" in Lake County. He wrote that law enforcement officials "hatched these charges against the three Negro boys because the family of the injured girl was so prominent in Lake County." Actually, the Davises were poor and ill-educated.

His series of articles won a major award from the American Newspaper Guild.

In an article for *The Nation*, a weekly political-opinion magazine published in New York City, Poston asserted that the trial was "a legal lynching" carried out by an all-white jury. "There was no medical testimony, no objective evidence like her clothes or the car in which the crime allegedly occurred. The word of one White girl was believed against that of three Negro youths who insisted that they had never seen her before."

In a later piece for *Editor and Publisher*, an authoritative periodical in the journalism field, Poston detailed an account of a personal experience while he was covering the trial in Tavares.

He said he had been pursued in his car from Lake County to Orlando "by a mob of angry White men" and only managed to escape them by driving at speeds of 80 to 90 miles an hour. He wrote that he had been denied protection from the sheriff's office.

The sheriff publicly challenged the assertions. He said Poston had asked him for a police escort and that he had told him it was unnecessary.

"Mainly, I think he wanted to be able to say he had to have a police escort to get out of the county safely. I told him that no one would bother him, and nobody did. I also told him that he came to Lake County unescorted, and without an invitation, and that he could get back the same way."

Poston also wrote that he personally had laid out all the facts of the Groveland rape case before U.S. Attorney General J. Howard McGrath.

Poston said Shepherd and Irvin were World War II veterans who had refused to work in the citrus groves for substandard wages.

Military records showed, however, that they both had spent
time in a federal prison and had been dishonorably discharged
from the army for separate crimes.

U.S. Army records specify that Shepherd was a private first
class attached to the 453rd Signal Heavy Construction Company
at Clark Field Army Air Base, in the Philippines, when he was
courtmartialed on December 31, 1947. Along with two other
soldiers, Shepherd was charged with violation of the 96th Article
of War – specifically, stealing three trucks. Shepherd and the two
other soldiers were convicted and sentenced to two years at hard
labor and a dishonorable discharge.

In a separate action at the same Army base, PFC Walter L.
Irvin was courtmartialed and sentenced to one year at hard labor
and a dishonorable discharge for illegal use of weapons in assembly with a group of other soldiers.

Irvin was dishonorably discharged Sept. 16, 1948, and Shepherd on March 2, 1949, according to the Army Records Admin-
istration Center in St. Louis, Missouri.

McCall, Hunter and several county officials contended that
the Poston articles and the grand jury investigation were solely
aimed at promoting the passage of civil rights legislation by the
U.S. Congress.

Hunter told reporter Ormund Powers of the *Orlando Sentinel,* "If Ted Poston were sincere in his attacks, he might be for-
given for being misinformed. But he is not concerned about the
race question in this case, only in creating dissension between the
races." Hunter said Poston "has begun a vicious campaign in the
Northern press against the people of the South, Lake County in
particular."

Williams, the NAACP's general counsel who had assisted
Akerman at the trial, wrote in the *Pittsburgh Courier* that the
whole Groveland affair was "part of a great plot to intimidate
Negroes in the community and force them to work for little or
no wages."

To that, Hunter angrily responded, ". . . They are not interested so much in justice for the Negro as they are in using him. By creating hatred between the North and South, they feel they will have a certain political advantage."

The prosecutor also took it upon himself to defend the actions of Lake County officials against then-Sen. Claude Pepper, a Florida Democrat, and *The St. Petersburg Times.*

The Florida newspaper wrote a series of articles which questioned the guilt of the defendants and the methods by which they had been brought to justice. It criticized the actions of county officials at the time of the riots. Since the popular senator was strongly supported by that newspaper, Pepper was asked by Hunter and others to repudiate the *Times.* Pepper refused.

This angered Hunter so much that he issued a public announcement that he would no longer support Sen. Pepper politically.

The prosecutor said he considered the articles "a libel upon the good people of Lake County." They followed the example of "the charges that have been made in the Northern press by a gang of radical New York lawyers and correspondents."

The prosecutor complained that for many months, the St. Petersburg newspaper "harassed, vilified and lied" about him, about Judge Futch, about Sheriff McCall and other citizens of Lake County. Hunter praised the sheriff, saying he acted "with great courage and tact to quickly quiet the mob spirit."

CHAPTER 12

GEOGRAPHICS, DEMOGRAPHICS AND SUCH

Although Florida is geographically part of the South, the Sunshine State's population and social attitudes, to name two factors, are varied mixtures not easily defined. One could devote a volume to the differences rather than similarities and how the whole admixture sometimes differs greatly — then and now — from the customs and attitudes of neighboring states.

But, I'll leave that to demographers, or academicians, or whoever studies such things.

The state's inhabitants are from many cultures, more so than most states, perhaps. Many of them arrived long after the Dixie traditions were commonplace, however, and they usually fit their own beliefs into the mainstream. Sometimes, these cultures clash, and one views the other as a strange interloper.

I am trying to avoid oversimplification, which is an injustice to the truth. This is certainly no treatise on racial issues, demographics or psychology. I am putting down what happened along with my, somewhat subjective, explanations of why these things took place.

The state has had some of the most prosperous and progressive areas in the nation, and some of the most backward. It has some of the best and worst aspects of the American character.

Those who call Florida home are a diverse lot, and they generally bring their cultures, beliefs and thinking to the fore when big issues arise. Lynching and blatant racism were in McCall's day big issues.

To me, the non-native Floridian is, and generally has been, different from a true southerner, or even a yankee. Recent immigrants are another story altogether, of course.

The Old South was part of Willis McCall's world, however. And that world was a tough one on the black citizen — for ever so many years after Civil War Reconstruction and Civil Rights Reformation.

Generally speaking, Sheriff McCall's "world" consisted of the wide, shimmering citrus belt extending east to west across the state's middle, and north almost to St. Augustine and Jacksonville. The latter, along with Tallahassee and Pensacola to the northwest, reach out to Georgia and Alabama and the rest of Magnolia Country.

At that time, Central Florida's Lake County was the world's No. 1 citrus producer.

In much of McCall's world, the basic and deeply held values revolved around a strong family, the church, local politics and government, patriotism and maintaining the *status quo.* These things were at the core of daily life in Lake County's small towns, and agricultural and ranching areas.

When someone messed with those values, he was meddling with life itself.

As an elected official, the sheriff had great influence and close ties to the people, a personalized bond which town cops and other county and state officials did not have. Even judges and prosecutors — though mainly local "boys" — did not have this familiar linkage. And the smaller the area, the closer the ties.

Some sheriffs used this familiarity to great advantage. The longer they were in office, the stronger their powers grew.

And McCall, in almost three decades, exercised awesome

power, often bordering on fear. Strangely, in my opinion, he may not have truly realized how much power he had.

CHAPTER 13

U. S. SUPREME COURT ORDER

The federal grand jury proceedings in Ocala were behind closed doors, as is usual under the law. But at their conclusion, the panel reported no civil rights violations against the three black defendants and returned no indictments. McCall offered to testify, but unexplainably, he was not called.

Shortly after that, the Florida Supreme Court upheld the convictions of Shepherd and Irvin. The Shepherd-Irvin lawyers took their appeal to the U.S. Supreme Court, which promptly reversed the state court's ruling and ordered the new trial.

Justice Robert Jackson, who wrote the court's powerful, nononsense opinion, noted that "newspapers published as fact, and attributed the information to the sheriff, that these defendants had confessed. No one, including the sheriff, repudiated the story. . . No confession was offered at the trial."

Justice Jackson wrote that the trial was "but a legal gesture to register a verdict already dictated by the press and the public opinion which it generated." He called it an example of "one of the worst menaces to American justice."

American justice should be protected by moving the trial elsewhere, "If freedoms of the press are so abused as to make fair trial in the locality impossible."

Florida Attorney General R.W. Erwin announced he was "very disappointed" by the Supreme Court's decision. Justice Glenn Terrell of the State Supreme Court said he was not surprised at the reversal. Back in Lake County, trial Judge Truman Futch shrugged and declined comment, and Hunter told reporters he didn't care where a retrial was held.

The blunt-spoken sheriff was not reticent in condemning the decision, however.

He disagreed with the finding that the press had influenced the verdicts. The trial jury's recommendation of mercy for Greenlee "is definite proof that the jury and court were impartial. The fact that they (defense lawyers) did not appeal the case of Greenlee along with the other two is an admission of guilt."

In his deceptively low-voiced manner, McCall said the U.S. Supreme Court had allowed the NAACP and similar organizations "to influence them to such a prejudiced extent that they saw fit to reverse one of the fairest and most impartial trials I have ever witnessed."

He accused the NAACP and reporter Ted Poston of "eloquent and sensational lies."

The sheriff declared he was shocked that the court would bow to such "subversive influences" and said the defendants' confessions were not used at the trial because there was plenty of other evidence to convict them.

While Shepherd and Irvin had won a new trial and arrangements were begun to return them to Lake County, Greenlee became the forgotten man in the case. After the initial trial, McCall disclosed that the teenager had admitted his part in the crime and had furnished details that were used at the trial. But Greenlee pleaded not guilty and was tried along with the other two.

"Let the defense lawyers explain that," he said.

After the trial, a corrections officer wrote a report in which he said the teenager admitted his guilt and had given him a detailed account of the crime. R.P. McLendon, who was a prison identification official, wrote out an account of what he said Greenlee told him at Raiford. It was typed and dated Sept. 17, 1949, and filed with Greenlee's prison records. It eventually emerged into the public realm. McLendon's report follows (as written except for the victim's name):

> "On Friday, July 15th 1949, subject and Ernest Thomas, residing in Gainesville (Thomas cooking at the Humpty-Dumpty Café) both hitch-hiked to Groveland, at which time Thomas was armed with a .45 Colt Revolver, arriving in Groveland about 4:30 PM, to visit Thomas's mother and father. About 9:30 subject and Thomas met their two accomplices, Samuel Sheppard (sic), No. 45539, and Walter L. Irvin No. 45540, at a Negro jook joint in Groveland, at which time Samuel Sheppard was driving his brothers automobile, a 1942 Mercury.
>
> "All four left Groveland and went to Clermont, stopping at a jook joint, later leaving Clermont, came back through Groveland on Highway No. 33, enroute to Leesburg.
>
> "Before arriving in Okahumpka, a motorist was parked on the side of the road, having car trouble. Subject and his three accomplices passed this motorist, who was having car trouble, going down the road a short distance turned around and coming back on the pretext of committing Armed Robbery, as suggested by accomplice Thomas.
>
> "Arriving back at the automobile, stopping, it was discovered that a White man and White woman were the only two people in the car, who later proved to be Mr. & Mrs. (Davis), man and wife. Accomplice Sheppard knocked Mr. (Davis)

to the ground, and accomplice Thomas hit Mr.
(Davis) also, and later they picked him up and
threw him over a fence, putting Mrs. (Davis) in
their car, and driving to Okahumpka, on Highway No. 33, turned left on Highway No. 48,
where later all four committed Armed Rape on
Mrs. (Davis), which took about forty-five minutes, subject being the last one to have carnal intercourse; Thomas was First, Irving was Second,
Sheppard was Third.

"After finishing the job they left Mrs. (Davis) near the edge of the Paved Highway (No.48),
soon after which Mrs. (Davis) was apparently
picked up by some passing motorist. Proper authorities were advised. Subject and his three accomplices returned to Groveland, at which time
they put subject out near the depot , inasmuch as
he had no place to sleep. Later, he was detected
sleeping in a packing shed by two nightwatchmen
connected with the packing house company, who
placed subject under arrest, at which time he was
armed with Thomas's .45 Colt Revolver.

"Later, it was revealed by officers and the
general public that this crime had been committed, at which time subject was questioned by the
authorities who immediately admitted his guilt.
Later the same morning, July 16th 1949, Sheppard and Irvin were arrested. Thomas made his
escape, and two or three weeks later was shot and
killed while resisting arrest, in the woods near
Madison, Florida.

"Subject was tried and convicted on the ensuing charge and received a Life Sentence, and he
calls himself a lucky person to receive only a life

sentence for the crime committed. Accomplices Sheppard and Irvin were sentenced to death."

McLendon's entry in the space for "crime" on Greenlee's record reads, "Rape White Female)."

Similar reports for Shepherd and Irvin either were not made by McLendon or other prison officials or they no longer exist in public records.

CHAPTER 14

SHERIFF KILLS ONE, WOUNDS ONE

Following the Supreme Court's scathing opinion of Lake County justice, Judge Futch set a hearing for November 7, 1951, to hear motions from attorneys for Shepherd and Irvin on a new trial date and location. The sheriff was ordered to bring the death row inmates back to Tavares for the hearing and retrial.

There was much angry talk in Lake County over the Supreme Court's decision, and McCall expressed concern that there might be a lynching party waiting. He took extra precautions for the nighttime transfer. He and Deputy Yates were the only ones who knew about the plan. The sheriff told prison officials that everyone else thought the prisoners would be transferred the following day.

Deputy Yates had earlier driven a car to Weirsdale, and on this night McCall dropped him off there on his way to Raiford.

When Shepherd and Irvin were handcuffed to each other and placed in the ample passenger side of the big car, the sheriff switched his .38 Special to his left hip, away from the prisoners as he drove. Much of the drive home was uneventful. McCall was in constant radio contact with his deputy.

The two prisoners became restless just as they got into Lake County, McCall said later. Just outside McCall's hometown of

Umatilla, about fifteen minutes from the Tavares jail, Shepherd and Irvin demanded that they be allowed out of the car to urinate.

At about the same time, the sheriff said he became aware of a steering problem with his car. Ignoring his passengers, he stopped, got out, looked around and saw that the left front tire was almost flat. Leaving the prisoners 'cuffed and in the car, he radioed Deputy Yates and instructed him to stop in Umatilla and get a gas station operator named Spence Rynerson to come out there as fast as he could to change the tire.

At that point, Shepherd and Irvin demanded they be let out of the car, McCall said. He quoted them, "If you don't let us get out and piss, we're going to wet all over your car."

Flustered and angry, the sheriff walked around and opened the door on the passenger side. "All right, damn it, get out and get it over with. I'm tired of you. I'm tired of listening to you."

"They got out of there and one of them suddenly hit me with (a big) flashlight on the side of the head," McCall testified later. "The other hollered, 'Get his gun.'"

The sheriff quickly pulled out his .38 Special and started shooting. Both prisoners went down. McCall told a county inquest jury later that week that Irvin "knocked hell out of me" with the three-battery flashlight that was sitting on the car seat.

"When he hit me, I fell down against the car. I was on one knee, and I fired that gun, first at one then the other. I emptied it, I surely did. If I had had any more than six shots in there I would still be shooting "cause I heard it click, click, click. . . I didn't know how many times I shot, back and forth to both men."

With both prisoners down, McCall radioed Yates again telling him what had just happened. He also reached the Tavares jail and instructed the dispatcher to contact a doctor and dispatch him to the site.

"I needed some help out there," he told the inquest jury later.

"I knew I was going to need some witnesses, too. Of course, nobody had seen it."

The shooting took place less than two miles from downtown Umatilla. The city council was in session when Deputy Yates burst in and informed the group. The meeting was quickly adjourned and everybody set out for the shooting scene.

On his way back, Yates also stopped in to tell Paul Bryan, a good friend of McCall's. Bryan was host that night in his home to a session of the Umatilla Kiwanis Club's board of directors. The sprawling Bryan homestead stands less than a quarter mile from the shooting scene just off County Road 450. The Kiwanis group quickly broke up and board members set out in the dark night to see what the shooting was all about.

It turned out to be quite a turnout for a tiny, quiet town in the middle of nowhere.

The first arrivals found a rumpled McCall, bleeding from one side of his face. He had on his suit coat but his white shirt was torn all the way down the front, exposing his ribbed undershirt. He was standing over the two black men, who were slumped over each other on the ground. Shepherd was dead. Irvin was alive, but he lay on the ground unattended until a doctor arrived.

Dr. Rabun Williams, the first physician on the scene, eventually administered an injection to Irvin until he could be transported to a hospital. But there was an additional wait when questions were raised over which ambulance service should transport a black man, and which hospital would accept him.

Also arriving at the dark shooting site were two other doctors, C.M. Tyre and Lawton Douglas.

The editor of the *Eustis Lake Regional News*, Marie Bolles, was the only newspaper reporter to go to the shooting scene that night. She was at her home in Umatilla when friends notified her. She and her husband, Glenn, drove out along the obscure country road as quickly as they could.

Some thirty people were there when she arrived, Mrs. Bolles reported. The bodies were still lying on the ground, sprawled across each other. The scene was lit by the headlights of several cars and one or two bobbing flashlights. The sheriff's car was half-way on the shoulder of the road.

"The Negroes were lying on their backs close to the car. There were no handcuffs on them." She could see blood oozing from Irvin's nose.

"Mr. McCall came up to me and said, 'Marie, it's just one of those things. I hate it that it happened.'"

She and her husband quickly took photos, trading off a bulky 4x5 Speed Graphic and flashbulbs. McCall was in disarray. The photos show the dark, grim scene, with the downcast McCall lit up by car headlights and the camera flash. He was agitated and kept prowling around, Mrs. Bolles said.

"I don't think Willis would have had it happen for anything," Mrs. Bolles said later. "He was trying to transport the prisoners quietly."

Irvin was in pain and groaning, and she could see the doctor giving him an injection.

"Shepherd had one shot through his head. I heard the other one had been shot three times. He was bleeding from his nose . . . I stayed at the scene for three-quarters of an hour. While I was still there, an ambulance came and took the two Negroes away."

Also part of the crowd was County Judge W. T. Hall, who immediately impaneled a coroner's jury on the spot. It consisted of Paul Bryan, John Nelson, Frank Robinson Jr., J.S. Allen Sr., L.T. Brennand and Mrs. Bolles. All were from Umatilla.

Amid the badly lit confusion, they took a close look at the physical evidence, including the nail-punctured tire and the body of Shepherd. But they made no official finding since the judge wanted McCall and Irvin to testify when they were able to do so.

After dealing with Irvin, Dr. Williams turned his attention to Shepherd. He verified that Shepherd died from the head wound. Dr. Williams then unfolded one of the dead man's clenched fists and found a small wad of hair. He took this and several other hairs sticking to Shepherd's jacket and carefully rolled them into a prescription blank, which he put into his pocket.

The doctors persuaded the shaken McCall to go to the hospital for observation for a possible concussion. Besides the cut on his left temple, the left lens on his eyeglasses was broken. Dr. Williams said the sheriff was in shock and that, because he had a heart problem, he would be checked for that, too.

Irvin was admitted to Waterman Memorial Hospital in Eustis. Doctors there stopped his internal bleeding and scheduled surgery later that week to remove a bullet lodged near his left kidney. McCall also was admitted for treatment and observation.

The following day, Attorney General McGrath ordered a Justice Department investigation of the shooting incident.

McGrath acted after front-page stories and broadcast reports about the shootings throughout this country and Europe. The attorney general also was prompted by demands from the NAACP and others asking that President Harry Truman order a probe into what the NAACP called "another case of summary Southern justice" against blacks.

The prisoner was kept incommunicado, under guard, in his hospital room for almost two days. Alex Akerman, his lawyer from Orlando, saw Irvin briefly on Wednesday but was prevented from talking to him by a deputy. The lawyer protested to the doctor, to Judge Futch, and indirectly to the sheriff. It did no good. He couldn't talk to his client until Thursday. The shooting took place Monday night.

"It is my opinion," Akerman told the press afterward, "that the only reasonable inference that can be drawn . . . is that as long as (McCall) can prevent it, he will not permit Irvin to tell his attorneys about the shooting incident, or the killing of Shepherd."

When Akerman was finally allowed to speak directly to Irvin Thursday evening, there was a court reporter there, along with a special investigator dispatched by the governor. Swathed in bandages and lying in his hospital bed, the wounded prisoner told a completely different story from that of the sheriff.

Irvin told his lawyer and the state investigator that the sheriff deliberately tried to kill him and Shepherd. While they were crumpled on the ground, Irvin said, Deputy Yates arrived. He soon discovered that he was not dead, and the deputy fired another shot at him.

Hoarse and laboring to talk because of a bullet wound to his neck, Irvin recounted that Sheriff McCall stopped the car near Umatilla to look at the tires. When he and Shepherd got out of the car, McCall just started firing, Irvin said.

The prisoner then was allowed to give a sworn statement to Akerman and Jefferson J. Elliot, special investigator for Gov. Fuller Warren. There were other onlookers in the suddenly crowded hospital room. The statement read, in part:

> "He (the sheriff) said, 'You sons of bitches get out and get this tire fixed.' I did not see any tires in back, but we had to obey because he was the sheriff. And we went to get out, and Shepherd he taken his foot and put it out of the car and was getting out, and I can't say just how quick it was, but he shot him, and it was quick enough. And he turned, the sheriff did, and he had a pistol, and shot him right quick, and then quick he shot me'"
>
> "Shot me right here (Indicating right upper chest) and he come on and when he shot me, he grabbed somewhere by my clothes and he snatched me.
>
> "He first shot Shepherd and that left me facing the face of the car, you know, the face of the car. Then he shot me, the time he reached me and grabbed me and snatched me, and Sammy too.
>
> "He snatched both of us and that threw both of us on the ground, and then I did not say anything. I didn't say nothing. So after he snatched

me, he shot me again, in the shoulder, and still I didn't say anything all that time.

"And I knew that I was not dead, and so I heard him say, 'I got rid of them. Killed the sons of bitches.' But still I didn't say anything.

"He ran around the car and called the deputy sheriff on the radio, and I heard him say, 'Pull around here right quick, these sons of bitches tried to jump me and I did a good job.'

"In about ten minutes, the deputy sheriff was there. He came from towards Umatilla and got out of his car and pulled his car over to the side of the road, and that pulled the car over to where the sheriff's car was parked, and the sheriff's lights were still burning.

"The deputy sheriff had a pistol. I don't know whether it was his pistol or the sheriff's pistol. And the deputy he shined the light in my face and he says to the sheriff, 'That son of a bitch is not dead.' And then he said, 'Let's kill him.'

"The deputy sheriff then pointed the pistol on me and pulled the trigger, snapped the trigger, and the gun did not shoot.

"And so he took it back around to the car lights and looked in it and shined the light in it and then something they said was about letting it stay cocked, so he turned it on me again and pulled it, and that time it fired, and it went through here (indicating the neck) and then I began to bleed and bleed out of my nose."

At that point, Akerman asked Irvin whether he was talking about Deputy Yates.

"Yes, sir. He shot me the third time. But I managed to pull through okay, 'Cause I did not say anything and did not let them know that I was not dead. And after all the people came – there was lots of people came there – and some of them predicted that I was not dead. I don't know whether they was all scared or what. Anyway, there was so many different people around there and they was all talking so it did not mean much to me.

"I heard some remarks that, 'He ought to have been dead long ago.'"

Akerman asked if he tried to "jump" the sheriff. Irvin replied he had not. He said he didn't try to escape because he "had no reason and had high hopes of coming out all right" at the second trial.

In answer, McCall curtly replied the following day, "I have made a statement and it is the truth. There is nothing more to say."

When informed of Irvin's allegations against him, Deputy Yates grinned and said, "It's a funny thing." That's all he would say.

Things moved quickly after that. Circuit Judge Futch directed that a grand jury be impaneled to determine the facts in the shooting. Governor Warren ordered another investigation. And County Judge Hall made plans to conclude the inquest he had begun at the scene of the shooting.

Akerman and Thurgood Marshall, chief counsel for the NAACP, issued a joint statement calling on the people of Lake County to demand justice for Shepherd and Irvin.

Voicing the doubts of many, Akerman asked about the shooting, "Why on that road? Why should he transport the prisoners himself? A lot of questions remain unanswered."

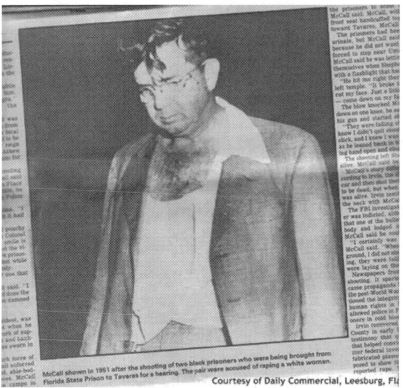

McCall shown in 1951 after the shooting of two black prisoners who were being brought from Florida State Prison to Tavares for a hearing. The pair were accused of raping a white woman.

A Disheveled Sheriff McCall – with glasses broken and shirt torn, the Central Florida official tells onlookers he shot to kill his two prisoners after they tried to escape from him. (Photo courtesy of Daily Commercial – Leesburg, Fla.)

CHAPTER 15

NAACP, THURGOOD MARSHALL, RUSSIA'S VISHINSKY

Thurgood Marshall — later to become a Supreme Court justice — became very active in the Florida case as attorney for the NAACP. He rushed to Lake County following the shooting, and he was in the hospital room when Irvin made his accusations against the sheriff and his deputy.

Also there was Special Agent Robert Wall, head of Miami's FBI office, who had been dispatched in response to the attorney general's call for a federal investigation. He was joined over the next several weeks by a score of federal and state investigators.

Also taking action was NAACP Executive Secretary Walter White, who telegraphed President Truman asking for a study of the case "by every appropriate government agency." He demanded that local authorities be prevented from "whitewashing" the shooting incident.

In New York, a convention of the one of the country's tops labor groups, the Congress of Industrial Organizations (the CIO) was informed of the case by Walter Reuther, president of the United Auto Workers Union. It was "not the first time a Negro prisoner was shot down because he was alleged to have tried to escape," Reuther said. In state after state, "where Negroes come before the Bar of Justice, there are two standards, one for Negroes and one for whites."

Reuther called upon both political parties to take immediate steps to carry out civil rights programs, adding his beliefs that Communists used such incidents for propaganda purposes. Sure enough, André Vishinsky joined the chorus by charging that the United States turned its back on human rights violations such as the case in Florida.

"This is what human rights means in the United States of America,' Vishinsky said after reading about the Lake County shooting in a newspaper in Paris. "This is the American life," he said, pointing to a widely used photograph of the scene in the paper.

The Soviet ambassador to the United Nations told French reporters that U.S. Secretary of State Dean Acheson had committed slander when he declared at the U.N. General Assembly earlier that week that Soviet satellite states were guilty of violating human rights. Vishinsky then said mockingly, if somewhat confusingly, "I think some people should look after their business before sticking their noses into other people's houses."

Asked about Vishinsky's statements, a restrained Marshall told Florida reporters that the case would obviously have an effect on this nation's role in the budding United Nations and on the nation's international prestige.

But, Marshall said, "If the state announces McCall has been arrested and indicted and will be vigorously prosecuted, that obviously will be an answer to what Russia might say. We know of no other answer that can be given."

The NAACP's White, in Daytona Beach for a meeting of the Florida chapter of the black organization, asserted that such incidents were "as valuable to Joe Stalin as would have been five or six divisions of well-armed, well-trained and well-equipped troops."

Listing other cases which had brought worldwide attention to this nation's racial problems, White declared that "the Jimmy

Byrneses, Herman Talmadges, Fielding Wrights and other Dix-
iecrats are doing infinitely more harm than all the Communists
in the U.S."

A group known as the Civil Rights Congress demanded
U.N. intervention "to end the continuing policy of genocide . . .
against the Negro people." It held a big protest rally in New York
against "this act of genocide by government."

The *Pittsburgh Courier*'s front page banner about the shooting read: SHOT DOWN LIKE DOGS. A one-paragraph bulle-
tin at the top of the lead story said Irvin had just been transferred
to Raiford prison because of "fear that Florida mobs might storm
Waterman Memorial Hospital."

The NAACP sent several special representatives to investigate
the case, besides keeping Marshall on a fulltime basis for the defense. Franklin Williams went on a speaking tour, raising money
and telling wild stories about prisoner beatings and threats supposedly made by McCall's people to him and other defense lawyers, and to reporters such as Poston.

Harry T. Moore, a leader in Florida's NAACP chapter, used
the movement to help increase membership and support. Moore
also pleaded for blacks to register and vote.

Meanwhile, McCall was basking under expressions of popular support from throughout the area. He received scores of cards,
letters and calls from his constituents and others. Many expressed
the same sentiment: They were lucky to have the sheriff stand tall
against Negroes, the NAACP, the communists and labor rabblerousers like Water Reuther.

The Tampa chapter of the Florida Peace Officers Association
awarded him a special commendation. Its chaplain, Baptist Min-
ister Lloyd King, asked, "What if this incident had happened in
reverse – that Sheriff McCall had been killed or nearly killed by
two Negroes? What would have been public reaction?"

Some supporters pointed out that those expressing so much
indignation over a sheriff killing a Negro had been virtually silent
when a Negro killed a sheriff earlier that year. They were right.

Sheriff Edward Porter Jr. of Marion County, adjacent to Lake County, was stabbed to death by a 16-year-old black youth when the sheriff questioned him about a bad check. The case caused little stir outside the state.

Said Charles Hahn Jr., executive secretary of the National Sheriffs Association: "Had the sheriff (McCall) been killed, he would have been a dead hero."

As for McCall, he told anyone who would listen, "If I had it all to do over, I'd do it again just the same way. I'm here and they're not. It could have been the other way around."

CHAPTER 16

PROSECUTOR, GOVERNOR, INQUEST JURY

Hunter, the brusque, chain-smoking prosecutor, had worked closely with McCall following the arrests in the Groveland rape case, during the trouble with the vigilante mobs and at the time of the trial and its aftermath. But he broke with the sheriff completely after the shooting of Shepherd and Irvin.

He called the shooting incident, "the worst thing that ever happened in Lake County."

There had earlier been some friction between the two county officials. Some saw it the result of McCall's popularity and Hunter's declining influence in the county, where he was used to calling the tune. According to this theory, Hunter now saw his chance to get rid of the sheriff, whom he believed was an embarrassment in the eyes of outsiders although a hero to Lake Countians.

The crafty prosecutor's methods became apparent not long after the shootings.

While he was still in a hospital bed, the sheriff had requested that Judge Futch appoint a representative from his office to any investigation since he was obviously an involved party. That didn't mean he was giving up his duties.

Hunter, though, wanted Gov. Warren to suspend the sheriff.

But he didn't publicly say so. Instead, the prosecutor told the governor privately that many citizens in Lake County were upset over the incident and wanted to meet with him. Hunter hinted strongly that many Warren supporters were among those who wanted McCall removed from office.

At the same time, the prosecutor told a group of prominent citizens of the county that the governor wanted a meeting to discuss the possible removal of McCall. This stirred the pot even more. As a result, two of the men went to the sheriff and warned him that Gov. Warren wanted him to resign, or at least step aside until after the investigations were concluded.

McCall was indignant.

"Hell no, I won't resign," he told the men. "I haven't done anything to resign for. If the governor doesn't want me in here, he'll have to fire me."

McCall eventually figured out what was going on and set up a meeting of his own with Gov. Warren. The governor denied he wanted to replace McCall. He said he had an open mind over the situation and would not take any action unless the sheriff was indicted. Satisfied with this, McCall returned home.

But Warren went ahead and met with the Lake County group, which was there on State Attorney Hunter's say-so. After the pleasantries, one of the group asked the governor why he had called the meeting. Surprised, the governor replied that he had been informed that the group wanted to meet with *him*. It soon became apparent that the prosecutor had set it all up. The parlay then broke up without any substantive discussion about McCall or the shootings.

So things went along that way until Saturday of that week. The inquest jury impaneled by County Judge Hall was reconvened, and Irvin, McCall, Yates and 14 others — doctors, law enforcement officers and townspeople — told their stories under oath.

Irvin again testified, painstakingly reiterating his earlier sworn statement that the sheriff killed Shepherd without provocation and then tried to kill Irvin. He said McCall fired twice at him at close range and Deputy Yates fired the third shot, trying to finish him off.

McCall and Yates denied the allegations.

"No one besides me shot them. I know my gun did it all," the sheriff testified. He said his deputy had not even been at the scene until his arrival with the Umatilla townspeople.

The sheriff testified he called Deputy Yates and later called his office "because I wanted as many people there as possible."

Yates told the inquest jury he first went to the Umatilla city hall, where the city council was in session, because he was trying to find a repairman to go out and fix the flat tire on the sheriff's car.

Before leaving city hall, Yates said he got a second radio transmission from the sheriff, telling him the prisoners had jumped him and that he had shot them, and telling him to get out there immediately. Deputy Yates said he rushed back into city hall and told everyone about the shooting. He then stopped off at Paul Bryan's house and told him McCall wanted him out there, too.

Yates said Mayor W.B. Calhoun arrived at the shooting scene before he did. Calhoun confirmed that the deputy showed up about five minutes after he had.

Gov. Warren's special investigator, Jefferson Elliott, testified next. He told the panel the sheriff's suit coat was "the best piece of evidence we have." The position of two powder burns on one sleeve "indicated the gun was fired during some kind of a struggle . . . He wasn't target-shooting."

Dr. Douglas said that when treating the sheriff later that night, he found the left side of his scalp "red and irritated-looking, and some of the follicles had hair missing. I assumed the hair had been pulled out by force." At the shooting scene, the doctor had taken pieces of hair from the dead man's clenched fist and several hairs that were stuck on Shepherd's coat.

But there was no further explanation and no follow-up on that testimony.

McCall had said Shepherd hit him once on the side of his face with the three-battery flashlight that was on the car seat. McCall didn't tell the inquest jury that he and Shepherd had physically struggled with each other. Irvin's testimony mentioned no physical struggle with the sheriff by either man.

The jury met for nine hours and deliberated for 30 minutes. It found the sheriff's actions were "justifiable by reason that Mc-Call was acting in the line of duty and in defense of his own life."

After the inquest verdict, two FBI men asked to come to the sheriff's house to take a sample of the sheriff's hair. McCall's young son Donnie was there and he was surprised by what he saw when one of the agents' pulled hair out of his father's head. "Daddy, why are you letting them do that?" he recalls saying.

The FBI officials also took the sheriff's flashlight, noting in their records that they found some hair under the screw-in portion. Whose, they didn't say. The agents also wrote that material from McCall's suit coat had been found mixed in with some taken from Shepherd's jacket.

To that, McCall joked, "I hope you know I wasn't hugging them sons of bitches 'cause I loved them. We had to be tussling for that to happen. We had a little tussle when he hit me."

After the inquest verdict, Irvin was transferred to the hospital at Raiford, this time under guard No charges were filed against him pending the results of the federal investigation and the Lake County grand jury probe.

CHAPTER 17

FEDERAL PROBE, RETRIAL FOR ONE

The federal investigation was still ongoing in February 1952 when a circuit court jury in Ocala convened to retry Irvin on the rape charge, as ordered by the U.S. Supreme Court. Whittlin' Judge Futch was again the overseer.

The crusty Futch had agreed to have the second trial moved to Ocala, a short drive north of Tavares but in a different county, Marion County. The defense had expected it to be held at a bigger venue such as Jacksonville or Miami. The defense may not have known that Marion County had in the past year undergone the experience of having its popular sheriff, Edward Porter Jr., stabbed to death by a teenage boy.

And since Marion County was still in the 5th Judicial Circuit, it remained under Futch's jurisdiction, and *he* became the presiding judge for the retrial, as he had been at the first trial!

The retrial of Walter Irvin took place at a time of violent racial strife throughout the country.

This time, Futch permitted the direct trial participation of Thurgood Marshall, plus another NAACP attorney, Jack Greenberg of New York City.

The judge overruled vehement objections by Hunter that the NAACP lawyers "represent an association of people outside the state engaged in a campaign of vilification against the courts and the people of the state of Florida."

Seven blacks were called as potential jurors but all were excused, four on findings by the court and three on challenges by Hunter. The courtroom was large but not filled. The balcony, however, was bulging with about 75 black spectators.

Mrs. Davis, now nineteen and the mother of a three-week-old baby, quietly repeated her story of the 1949 rape.

Hunter described Irvin's accuser as "an honest Cracker girl, poor, upright and never in any trouble." He said she and "her ol' country husband were riding on a peaceful Lake County road where every person should be secure."

Irvin, now the lone defendant, nervously but firmly denied that he knew Thomas or Greenlee. He testified he had been out drinking beer with Sam Shepherd at several clubs in Groveland and Orlando on the night of the crime. He did not get into a fight with a white man or kidnap and assault a white woman, he said.

"I never have commited rape. I am not guilty," he repeated before stepping down from the stand.

Among those attending the trial were Shepherd's parents, Henry and Charlie Mae Shepherd, and his brother James, who were then living in Orlando.

In an eloquent plea for "fairness and Justice," Thurgood Marshall described the case as "the acid test of constitutional, law" under which "the wealthiest and most influential citizen gets no better treatment than the poorest sharecropper."

Quoting the late Justice Harlan, Marshall declared, "The Constitution is color blind."

It was a 15-minute argument and Marshall's only direct participation in the trial. He was "very conservative in court," said reporter Emmett Peter. "He didn't dwell on the race issue like Williams."

The 12-man jury found Irvin guilty of rape, and Judge Futch

again sentenced him to death. Some of the friends and relatives in the now-overflowing balcony wept.

In November, 1952, a year after the sheriff shot Shepherd and Irvin, the federal grand jury, meeting in Jacksonville, cleared the sheriff and Deputy Yates of any civil rights violations in the shooting incident.

When it met for the final time, the 22 person panel, which included one black man and one black woman, spent two days listening to testimony. It then returned a "no true bill," indicting no one. It heard 23 witnesses, including Irvin, three FBI investigators, doctors Williams and Douglas, County Judge Hall and many of the local people who had gone to the scene of the shootings that night. Also questioned closely was Dr. George E. Englehard, from Leesburg, who testified for 45 minutes about his autopsy on Shepherd.

Under the law, federal grand jury proceedings are held behind closed doors and jurors and witnesses are under oath not to reveal any of their testimony. As usual, however, some of the details leaked out.

One surprising development was the testimony of three state prison inmates, who told the jury they heard Shepherd and Irvin plotting to escape from the sheriff before they were picked up for their return to Lake County. This was the first substantial report of its kind, although there had been rumors about that earlier.

In an effort to determine the basis for such testimony, I later turned up two letters referring to the alleged prison-hatched scheme.

First, Sheriff McCall wrote the governor on January 3, 1952, asking a temporary stay in the scheduled execution of death row inmate James Leivy a few days hence, on January 7. (The correct spelling of his last name was Leiby). McCall wrote that Leiby had already given a statement to the FBI. But, said the sheriff, "I believe that testimony from him in person would have great bearing in the case should the prejudiced groups in New York bring enough pressure to bear in Washington for the Justice Department to place this case before a Federal Grand Jury."

The second letter to the governor about the case was from R. P. McLendon, director of the State Prison's Bureau of Identification. It also was dated January 3, 1952. McClendon was the same officer who took Greenlee's statement on his arrival at the prison in September 1949. According to McClendon, Greenlee had admitted to the rape at that time and implicated Shepherd, Irvin and Thomas in the case.

Now, in January 1952, McClendon was writing the governor that he had been present on December 4, 1951, when two FBI agents interviewed all eight condemned men in the death house. The purpose of the interview was to determine if Shepherd and Irvin had made any statements "that would substantiate McCall's actions" in the shooting incident.

Further, McClendon wrote the governor, that prisoner, James Merlin Leiby, told the FBI that Irvin had purchased a nickel-plated cigarette lighter, which could be used in an escape attempt after they were returned to Lake County for retrial. There was no mention of such a lighter in Irvin's possession the night of the shooting.

McLendon further wrote, "He (Leiby) made other complementary statements, which I think proves Sheppard (sic) and Irvin left here with full intentions of making their escape, and that Sheriff McCall acted in self-defense. . .

"Leiby was told by FBI agents that no doubt their full report would be presented to the federal district attorney of Tampa (the grand jury prosecutor), and he (Leiby) along with others would probably be subpoenaed before the federal grand jury to substantiate the full statement made by him.

"This evidence is not known to the press," continued McLendon," but no doubt will come to life when such is known to the federal grand jury."

The available records reflect no response from the governor to the correspondence, but Leiby *was* given a reprieve from the electric chair and testified before the grand jury in Jacksonville. There was no other explanation as to why Leiby was speaking out now.

Leiby, from Frederick, Maryland, was sentenced to die for killing traveling companion Leonard Appplebaum, a Baltimore pharmacist, and hiding his body under a bridge in the Everglades.

Other accounts disclosed that two other death house inmates testified before the grand jury. What they said or how much credence was placed in the testimony is not known.

McCall offered to testify but was, unexplainably, not called.

Robert E. Duckett, an FBI agent from Washington D.C, testified about laboratory studies conducted from evidence in the case. He introduced a cardboard box containing lab samples of materials taken from the clothing of Shepherd, Irvin and McCall, from Shepherd's body and from the ground at the shooting site. Presumably, the sheriff's hair samples and their analysis were also included.

The Justice Department investigation was headed by Herbert S. Phillips, the U.S. Attorney in Tampa, who led the same type of probe after the prisoners' arrests in 1949, and Ben Brookes of the U.S. Attorney General's office in Washington. Presiding was U.S. District Judge Bryan Simpson.

Several grand jurors commented later that it was "a very tough case" and that the panel had voted overwhelmingly but not unanimously in favor of the sheriff. Why McCall was not called before the grand jury was not explained by anyone.

The same jury also considered a second case: a civil rights complaint lodged against Lake County's prosecutor, Jesse Hunter. This was a surprising development. The state attorney was accused of holding a black prisoner in jail for more than a year. Hunter was indicted by the jury panel after it determined that he had deprived David McKenrick Reese of his liberty without due process of law.

Judge Simpson explained that Reese and another black man,

William Timmons, had been tried on charges of first degree murder in Brooksville in July 1950. Timmons was convicted and Reese acquitted. However, Hunter asked that Reese be held in jail pending further investigation into other charges. The request was granted by the trial court.

The prosecutor then forgot all about Reese.

A reporter found the prisoner still in jail some nineteen months later. The Justice Department brought the case to the same grand jury which heard the McCall case. Ironically, the sheriff was cleared while the prosecutor was in hot water, albeit over a different case.

Hunter was scheduled for trial in Tampa, But in September 1953, Judge Simpson dismissed the charge, concluding that the matter was outside the jurisdiction of the federal government. He said inmate Reese should have taken his case to a state court.

Less than a year after that, a federal appeals court upheld Simpson's ruling and the case was dropped.

CHAPTER 18

COMMUTATION AND NOTORIETY

Walter Irvin's second conviction and sentence were upheld by the Florida Supreme Court. The U.S. Supreme Court denied an appeal to review the case a second time.

This then precipitated a campaign to commute Irvin's death sentence. And, as with everything else connected to the case, it brought to the fore strong emotions, bitter words and allegations of wrongdoing on both sides of the issue.

The era was one of increasing violence against black citizens throughout the nation.

Dynamite became a favorite terrorist tool in the 1950s in Florida. A housing development for black tenants in Miami was bombed twice. The Miami Hebrew School, a Roman Catholic church and a Jewish synagogue also suffered damage from explosives. The blasts came to be called "hatebombs."

A Christmas Night explosion in 1951 ended the lives of Harry and Harriet Moore at their home in the quiet little town of Mims, a short distance from Lake County. Harry T. Moore, a schoolteacher and former president of the Florida NAACP, had been a prominent fund-raiser for Walter Irvin's appeal and commutation of sentence. The bomb was planted under the Moores' bedroom and exploded as they were retiring for the night.

There were numerous other hate crimes in the state and around the nation at that time. To mention a few, a youth named Willie Vincent, was beaten and tossed from a car driven by whites. Another black, Melvin Womack, was dragged from his bed by four masked white men, beaten and shot to death. His body was found in a Central Florida orange grove.

Ebony, a prominent nationwide magazine primarily intended for blacks, described the hate crimes as coming from a willful white minority. "They operate as individuals rather than as mobs. Encouraged by lax police and bigoted politicians, they have flouted the law in their attempts to turn back the clock. . . "

The commutation campaign for Walter Irvin was led by a group of 50 churches called United Churches of Greater St. Petersburg (Florida) Its executive secretary, the Reverend Ben F. Wyland, was at the forefront of the effort and raised a storm of criticism in Lake County when he formally petitioned Gov. LeRoy Collins to throw out the death sentence.

The NAACP and Committee of 100 were active in the fight to keep Irvin out of the electric chair, too. The Committee coupled its appeal with letters soliciting financial contributions to help defray a total of $50,000 spent by NAACP lawyers over the years.

"Should Walter Irvin go his death, he will go an innocent man," said a committee letter sent out to those solicited for money. "He has refused three times to accept an offer of a life sentence on the condition that he plead guilty."

Committee Chairman Allan Knight Chalmers said in the letter he had "personally and repeatedly" investigated the evidence and determined that the prisoner was innocent and would not have been brought to trial had he not been a Negro.

Angered by the movement, McCall mounted a letter-writing campaign of his own, including a missive to the governor trying to head off a favorable decision by the Florida Board of Pardons to the petition for commutation.

"The courts of justice have spoken," McCall wrote Gov. Collins.

"Irvin has twice been indicted by grand juries. Twice, 12 men have seen fit to find him guilty without recommendation of mercy. He has twice been sentenced to the electric chair. This conviction upheld both times by the Florida Supreme Court. . . Upon hearing so-called new evidence, the U.S. Supreme Court saw fit to again confirm action of the lower courts. . . In my opinion and the opinion of many other citizens of this state, especially this section, it would be a gross miscarriage of justice for Irvin's sentence to be commuted to life imprisonment with the possibility of later being pardoned."

The sheriff criticized the NAACP's role in the campaign.

"Should they accomplish this goal, it would mean one thing. That all a Negro criminal would need to do would be to pick out some innocent helpless White woman as a target to satisfy his ravishing sexual desires, keep his mouth shut, proclaim his innocence and let the NAACP furnish the money and lawyers and beat the rap. . ."

Gov. Collins and the Pardons board were unmoved by the arguments of the sheriff and others who believed similarly. In January 1956, they commuted the death sentence and moved Irvin off death row.

This so angered the normally placid Judge Futch, who had presided at both trials, that he impaneled a Lake County grand jury to investigate the governor's action. The evil hand of Communism was brought into the issue. Documents to the grand jury stated that the Communist Party "meddled with the discretion of high public officials of this state."

Also at issue was whether Mrs. Davis had signed a petition opposing capital punishment. She appeared before the panel and said she had not. McCall wrote the governor the rape victim had signed a petition she believed opposed U.S. action in the Korean War.

Judge Futch said he expected the grand jury to call the governor and members of the Board of Pardons to testify.

There was no official summons, but the governor told reporters he would refuse to appear because it would set a precedent in relations between the executive and judicial branches of government. There the issue died.

The Groveland rape case was finally over for Willis McCall. But this was only in a legal sense. In reality, the sheriff would never be rid of it.

One way or another, the principals in the case left it behind them and went on with their lives. The Davises continued to live quietly in Lake County.

The NAACP lawyers, Thurgood Marshall and Franklin Williams, moved into positions of increasing prominence as America went through the turbulent years of the civil rights movement. Akerman went back to his practice in Orlando, The judge and prosecutor were not greatly affected one way or another.

Irvin was eventually released from prison. He died in 1969. Greenlee also was paroled and faded quietly into the mainstream never to be heard from again. Samuel Shepherd and Walter Thomas were dead.

But McCall was left with . . . what? Notoriety. The historical record. The case made him famous, or infamous, depending on the point of view. Right or wrong, he acquired a reputation as a tough, no-holds-barred lawman who ruled his part of the world according to his own conceptions of right and wrong.

Despite coroners' inquests, two grand juries, two trials, the FBI investigations – all legally justifying his actions – McCall and his version of *lawandorder* were now and forever open to question and criticism.

Having first shielded two Negro prisoners from a lynch mob by hiding them out in his home, he later shot and killed one and tried to kill the other, leaving him seriously wounded, in a nighttime shootout in which he had the only gun.

He did this during a period when blacks were just beginning to establish their rights in the postwar period of America's emerging social consciousness. He had done this in Lake County, Florida, a Southern backwater which some came to see as a microcosm of "Southern Injustice."

The liberal white activist, the daring black seeking social change and respect, many average Americans, would find it easy to stereotype and condemn a sheriff like McCall.

It would become easy and popular for journalists to point to this big, outspoken Lake County sheriff and make him a caricature of what Southern lawmen were all about.

The Groveland Rape Case, and his leading role in it, would forever be part of the background story of the long reign of Sheriff Willis V. McCall.

CHAPTER 19

YOUNG MCCALL, FIRST ELECTION

It can be quite an elucidating experience to look into the background or early life of someone who goes on to do extraordinary things.

You often wonder and think. now wait a minute! Where did this larger-than-life character come from? Was he always a big shot? Did he ride horses and shoot guns before he became sheriff? Was he always a big kid throwing his weight around in school? Just what did he do way back there in his early years?

Some of this may come out in an election campaign, but that could be only the tip of the iceberg, really, especially in small-town politics.

So, here it is, as briefly as I can make it.

As a kid, McCall lived on a farm and his first-paying job was trapping gophers for cash. He milked cows, raised chickens and a little bit of hell, it appears. He worked in his father's restaurant for awhile as a teenager.

Willis Virgil McCall was born July 21, 1909, at his grandparents' house on the shore of Lake Omega, near Umatilla. The grandparents had homesteaded there since shortly after the Civil War.

Willis was one of four boys born to Walter and Pearl Mc-

Call. Two of the boys died young. The McCalls also had two daughters. And Walter McCall brought to the marriage another daughter, borne by his first wife before she died in a fire.

Willis' father was a farmer, timber contractor and citrus-crew boss. The McCall farm was in pine woods and palmettos about three miles down a dirt road from that of Pearl's parents, on the bank of Mill Creek. The McCalls' nearest neighbors lived about a mile away, down another dirt road.

One of Willis' first memories was of helping his father put down straw on the road from Eustis to the hamlet of Messina. The road was a mail route, and the job consisted of dumping and packing pine needles into the sand ruts to keep it passable. The same thing was done throughout much of the area. There were no paved roads in Lake County at that time, although some of the towns had clay streets.

Willis got his first job when he was seven, trapping gophers for his dad, who would store them and then sell them to a man who came by once a week from St. Augustine. Willis got a nickel apiece for them, and his dad sold them for a dime. Farm people would use gophers in soup, and the small burrowing animal would make a tasty hash when mixed with potatoes and onions.

The brothers and sisters chopped and picked cotton, raised chickens, milked cows and tended a vegetable garden. Willis peddled vegetables after school for spending money.

He walked about three miles to a one-teacher school in Seneca every day for three years. As the children got older, the father sold the farm and bought another one closer to Umatilla so that the kids could attend the town schools.

Ever the entrepreneur, young Willis saw a chance to make some good money as soon as he was old enough to drive. Since the county school board didn't operate a bus system, it paid families with schoolchildren five dollars a month for each child's transportation to school. So with the help of his father, Willis purchased a Model-T Ford and began transporting his two sisters and brother, plus seven other kids from surrounding farms, to school. For eleven students, including himself, he collected the princely sum of fifty-five dollars every month.

He paid off the car and had some spending money left over after expenses for gas, oil and an occasional tire or battery. He could get seven gallons of gas for a dollar.

After his high school graduation in 1927, Willis ran a restaurant his father had bought in Umatilla. But then he decided that wasn't his line of work and went off to see some of the world with two friends, Gilbert Crow and Ned Smith.

They went to Virginia, Colorado and Wyoming, working at odd jobs for five months, until this trio of Florida Crackers was abruptly introduced to snow and bone-chilling cold weather. They hurried off to Los Angeles, where they stayed another two months and then started working their way home. They were gone from Florida for about a year.

Casting about for something to do back home, Willis took over three or four milk cows and some heifers from his father. Every day of the week, he would get up early, do the milking and then drive around town peddling it. He was soon visited by a dairy inspector, who informed him he needed to follow certain health measures and lay a concrete floor in the barn if he wanted to continue to sell milk commercially.

Willis decided he might as well go into the dairy business in a big way. He made the necessary improvements, purchased some more cattle and ran the prospering business from 1930 to 1935, when he sold it to go to work for the state Department of Agriculture as a citrus fruit inspector. He was twenty-six years old.

During this period, Willis married a local girl, Doris Daley.

"Oh, he wasn't an angel," his maternal grandmother told a curious Doris when they were courting. "He was sometimes way ahead of some of the other kids his age, but he had his devil-may-care ways about him, too. Adventure, challenge of some sort! He always wanted that."

In 1931, the McCalls had the first of three sons.

As a fruit inspector, Willis worked in packinghouses in different areas of Florida's wide citrus belt. In the offseason, he traveled to other states on similar assignments for the Federal-State Inspection Association, inspecting watermelons and peaches in Georgia, and apples, tomatoes and cherries in Pennsylvania.

It was enjoyable work. He made numerous friends among the growers, packinghouse owners and employees. But after nine years, Willis and Doris McCall tired of moving from place-to-place. Their oldest son, Malcolm, had been to four different schools. By the time they were assigned back to Eustis, McCall had resolved to find some other line of work and stay in his native Lake County.

He was 34 years old and wanted something better in life.

About this time, Sheriff Balton A. Cassady died in office, and McCall asked himself a fateful question: Why not run for sheriff?

The field was wide open. His present job had minor aspects of law enforcement to it. The McCall name was known around the county, especially since his Uncle Frank (Buck) McCall had been a recent candidate for the Florida Legislature and had come close to being elected. Adding to the name-recognition factor, Willis reasoned, was the popularity of *McCall's Magazine*, which also sold women's dress patterns under that name, a highly sought item among farm wives in those days. Of course, Willis had nothing to do with either, but having the same name didn't hurt.

He figured he had nothing to lose.

He started making the rounds and asking some of his friends and neighbors what they thought of the idea.

Postmaster Alex Morrell told him bluntly that he didn't have a chance. He could find better uses for his money than a political campaign. A friend, Robert Collins, told him to forget about it.

But others encouraged him.

Citrus grower and shipper Bill Shriner told McCall he would pay his filing fee if he ran. C.A. Vaughn, owner of a citrus packinghouse, said he had a good chance against the field. A boyhood friend, C. V. Griffin, prospering in real estate and citrus, offered financial help.

Vaughn would often tell the story about coming home and informing his wife that McCall wanted to run for sheriff.

"Well, if he runs, I'll vote for him," she said.

That decided it for Vaughn. "That's the first time in our married life she hadn't asked me who to vote for. By golly, I decided right then if my wife was going to vote for him, I better get out and work for him."

So McCall entered the race. Suddenly, it became a crowded field. The office was a good one, and the pay wasn't too bad. Five other men entered the Democratic primary race in 1944.

At that time, Florida Democrats didn't worry too much about Republican political opponents, if any there be. The nomination was tantamount to election, if the winner had a clear majority. Anything less meant a second primary, or runoff election. In a crowded field, 50 percent-plus-one would not be an easy feat.

McCall was the only one wearing a hat for his campaign picture, in this case a snap-brim fedora, which along with a dark suit and flashy smile gave him the look of a whimsical Phillip Marlowe, private eye.

He threw himself into the campaign, calling on old friends and citrus industry people, speaking at any public gathering and going door-to-door — his large, stocky frame, soft voice and polite manner surprising and captivating many of those who met him for the first time.

One of his opponents told a story about Ol' Willis "being over to Leesburg campaignin' and kissin' babies fast and furious until he realized that they was being handed to him upside down."

It was that kind of political race, fun and friendly-like.

McCall led the ticket. In a county with a population of about 28,500 and some 8,000 registered voters in 26 precincts, he garnered 1,563 votes to the 1,458 registered by H.P. Pryor Jones, a druggist in Leesburg. They had defeated the Clermont police chief, C.E. Sullins; the chief deputy under the deceased sheriff, Clarence Cooper; a former police chief of Eustis, Al Hammonds; and farmer Clyde Revels.

McCall and Pryor Jones ran an amicable campaign in the runoff primary, praising each other and trying not to antagonize any of their mutual friends. Jones' brother, Earl, a grocer, told McCall that if his brother wasn't a candidate, "I'd sure vote for you."

Pryor Jones told this humorous story to a group of supporters:

"I was down to Mascotte campaignin' the other day and I saw this old lady over at a woodpile choppin' wood. I figured I'd get her vote so I toted that wood in the house for her. When I got in there and put the load of wood down, there sat Ol' Willis over behind the stove a-churnin' butter."

McCall defeated Jones by 447 votes.

He inherited a department consisting of two deputies, a jailer, a matron (the jailer's wife) and a secretary-bookkeeper.

He went into the job on the first day of January 1945. "I went in cold turkey. I saw it as a challenge. But I felt I was the best man for the job." He was thirty-five, the youngest sheriff in the state at that time.

McCall and his two deputies were covering a land area of more than 1,000 square miles. They had no radio communication for the first couple of years. Complaints came in by telephone or from somebody walking in the door.

His salary was $5,000 a year, plus a percentage of the fees set down by law for specific duties such as arrests, court appearances, commitments, process serving and so on. The maximum he could earn was $7,500 under the fee system, and the first year he earned $6,000. During his second term, the legislature started basing sheriff's salaries on each county's population.

CHAPTER 20

LABOR UNIONS, ORANGE PICKERS
AND COMMIES

The new sheriff's first controversial case had to do with an agricultural union's recruiting efforts among Lake County citrus pickers, primarily blacks who harvested oranges on a piecework basis every season.

The activity was part of a more general union movement throughout the citrus belt. It was organized by a group called the Florida Citrus Workers Council, which decided to move in after growers and packinghouses cut the payment for each harvested box of oranges from fifteen cents to twelve.

A young labor organizer, Eric Axilrod, came into Lake County from Texas via Dade City, Florida, to sign up citrus harvesters for the Food, Tobacco, Agricultural and Allied Workers Union of America (FTA-CIO).

The growers said the reduction in pay was necessary because of the low price the fruit was getting in the fresh-fruit market. They pointed out that good harvesters could still make 10 to 12 dollars a day. Many of the men, women and children harvesting the fruit off the trees and hauling it to packinghouses objected.

The FTA stepped in and declared a long "Easter Holiday,"

during which organizers worked to sign up new members and force the growers to pay more money.

The union urged pickers to stay out of the groves to protest the lower price-per-box. Company trucks making the rounds for workers were soon coming back to groves and packinghouses virtually empty. There were reports that some workers were staying home because they feared reprisals from union organizers.

Axilrod and other labor leaders distributed thousands of handbills urging workers to stand firm and stay out of the groves until they got more money.

One of the circulars pictured a black harvester holding a box of oranges in one hand and a loaf of bread in the other. "Twelve-Cent Oranges Won't Buy One Loaf of Bread," it read. "Don't Starve Tired."

Union sympathizers and those opposed to union activities clashed at several rallies.

McCall jumped into the middle of it with his shiny cowboy boots. He began touring the Negro neighborhoods, asking the residents to return to work, promising protection for those who claimed they were afraid.

The county's largest industry was being brought to a standstill, and McCall was trying to get it moving again. Critics said he was just the doing the work that the citrus industry had elected him to do: force the blacks to stay in the groves at shockingly low wages.

The sheriff broke up a union meeting in Leesburg, accusing organizers of plotting violence. When he heard that Axilrod was conducting another rally in Mount Dora, he asked the police chief to detain the labor leader until he got there. McCall then drove over and arrested Axilrod on charges of intimidation. The sheriff accused the union official of threatening to "shoot Negro workers out of the (citrus) trees" if they reported to work during the harvesting holiday.

He hauled Axilrod in handcuffs before knots of workers standing around in confusion and demanded: "Does he look to you like he's going to shoot anybody out of the trees? This fellow isn't going to shoot anybody. If there's any shootin' going on, I'm gonna be in the middle of it."

From behind bars, Axilrod denied intimidating or threatening harvesters. He said the union would "continue to organize those workers who want to be organized under the laws of Florida."

John G. Lackner, international representative for the FTA, fired off a telegram to the sheriff demanding that he study federal statutes permitting labor organization "before you incur further liability within your jurisdiction for possible violations of these laws."

Enjoying the fray, McCall immediately replied with a terse wire of his own, suggesting that Lackner look up Florida laws prohibiting intimidation of workers.

The sheriff said he was not opposed to union meetings or attempts to organize labor by orderly means but, "I will do all I can to prevent organized labor from intimidating free labor. Labor unions cannot get away with terrorism in this county."

The state attorney made some allegations of his own.

Hunter called the union "a Communist outfit which is trying to scare the Negroes into joining." he repeated the sheriff's contention that Axilrod had told the pickers they would be shot from the trees if they returned to the groves to pick oranges at the twelve-cent scale.

The Florida Citrus Workers Council retaliated by dropping leaflets throughout the area from airplanes. Featuring a caricature of a snorting McCall holding a club, the handbills accused the sheriff of using Gestapo tactics "to coerce, intimidate and drive workers back to their cut–rate jobs."

The mimeographed documents were headed: MCCALL AGAINST THE LAW.

The handbills claimed the sheriff had invaded and interfered with an open public meeting in Leesburg without specific charges or warrants. He used his position "like a Kangaroo Court in which he was prosecutor, judge and jury — as well as sheriff."

McCall arrested Axilrod and seven other citizens who were not formally charged but told to get out of the county "and never come back, or else."

The angry sheriff called the union organizers Communist-inspired racketeers who were trying to scare workers into joining them. "People like that are not welcome in Lake County. They have sold their American heritage down the river to a bunch of Communists for a price."

After several days in jail, Axilrod was released to the custody of his father, a businessman from Dallas. He forfeited a $1,000 bond by deciding to leave the state. McCall's deputies tailed his car north, through the Florida Panhandle and into Alabama.

The WTA's recruiting efforts fell apart, and the pickers went back to work at the growers' wages. But the union declared it would try to prevent McCall's reelection.

In a letter to Dade County Solicitor Robert Taylor, union official H.C. Walton of Miami complained of McCall's actions in jailing Axilrod and "stopping the workers of Lake County from joining the CIO at a time when they were fighting a 20 percent wage cut." He accused McCall of throwing up "a big red scare in trying to hide the illegality and one-man campaign of intimidation which he was conducting."

Walton said the FTA-CIO would fight McCall "to see that he is defeated in the coming election."

Whatever the effort, it wasn't enough.

In fact, McCall's iron-fisted efforts against the unionists were so highly thought of, he was re-elected in 1948 by a two-to-one margin over his primary opponent, Clyde R. Revels, a Leesburg watermelon dealer.

He considered the Axilrod-union episode a personal triumph.

The experience hardened his conservative views and gave rise to his suspicions that Communists were out to create mischief wherever they could, including his own territory.

His easy reelection and his increasing popularity strengthened his conviction that — along with crime-solving — his job was to protect the citizens of Lake County from undue influences both from within and from the outside. The Communist menace must be dealt with severely, and he set out to do just that.

CHAPTER 21

WHITES, BLACKS OR INDIANS?

Allen Platt, a slight, dark-skinned man of Croatan Indian descent, made a decent living as a cotton farmer in Orangeburg County, South Carolina, for many years. But the going got rough in 1954.

Platt and his brother were barely making ends meet that year, coping with drought, government allotments and falling prices. Instead of the 25acres they had planted the year before, they could now plant only five.

Reluctantly, Allen Platt and his wife Laura decided they would have to give up farming. There just wasn't enough money in it to support their seven children. The Platts' two older boys had found jobs in Charleston, but after expenses they had little money to send home.

The family decided to listen to the advice of friends: Why not go to Florida? They could make a living there and improve their lives.

So the Platts and their seven children decided to leave their native South Carolina and move to Mount Dora, a handsome, lakeside community in Lake County.

The placid village had been patterned after many of the small towns in New England. It was a big town by Lake County standards, about 4,000 residents. Many well-to-do-Northerners maintained winter homes there; others were finding it a perfect place to retire. President Calvin Coolidge had found it an oasis from the wintertime rigors of Washington, sunning, swimming and boating in Lake Dora while staying at the sprawling Lakeside Inn.

Platt and his teenage sons — Rutledge, Denzell and Raymond — arrived in Mount Dora in September, 1954, leaving Mrs. Platt and their daughters temporarily in South Carolina. The father rented a house on Highland Street and found a job.

Less than a week later, Platt enrolled Raymond, then15, in the Mount Dora Fifth Avenue School as an eighth grader. Rutledge, who was 19, and Denzell, 17, were no longer attending school. They were workingmen like their father and also had found jobs in the area. The following weekend, Allen Platt decided to return to South Carolina with Rutledge to relocate the mother and daughters.

Denzell and Raymond remained in Mount Dora that weekend, and the teenagers decided to go to a movie in nearby Eustis on Saturday night. In the middle of the film, a woman sitting behind Denzell in the theater suddenly left her seat, strutted up to the front lobby and indignantly asked for the manager. She told him angrily that there was a colored youth in the theater, sitting in the row right in front of her.

The woman pointed to the offender in the darkened theater. The manager then tapped Denzell on the shoulder and asked him to accompany him to the lobby. There, the manager told Denzell there had been a mistake and he would have to leave since the theater didn't permit Negroes to attend.

Protesting that he was not a Negro, the bewildered 17-year-old reached in his pocket and from a worn billfold extracted a tattered copy of a birth certificate which attested that he was white. The family members had learned over the years to carry such copies to head off any infrequent racial questions. The boys' parents and their families were Croatan Indians from the Carolinas, and some of their forebears had been Irish.

But the manager wouldn't be swayed and insisted that the youth and his brother leave the moviehouse.

The incident was recounted when the rest of the family arrived in Mount Dora. But the Platts knew better than to make an issue of it and decided to ignore it.

"I trained my children to go to Sunday school, not to movies," said Laura Platt. "I told them they could go to no more movies."

The theater incident would have been forgotten except for what happened soon after that.

During the following week, the Platts enrolled their daughters in the Fifth Avenue School. Thirteen-year-old Laura Belle, who had been virtually a straight-A student back in Orangeburg, started to classes within two days after her arrival in Mount Dora. The younger girls – Esther, 10, Linda, 9, and Violet, 6 – followed a few days later.

A week after they started in school, Principal D.D. Roseborough went to see McCall in the sheriff's office in Tavares. The school principal explained that he was receiving complaints from parents of other students about the new arrivals, the Platts.

"He told me that some of the parents were convinced the Platt kids were Negroes, or at least had Negro blood, and they didn't want their children associating with them or attending class with them," McCall said. "He was being harassed, and the Platt kids were being harassed."

So McCall decided to pay a call on the Platts. Accompanied by Roseborough and a deputy with a camera, he went to the Platt home that evening.

Mrs. Platt was alone with her children. The sheriff didn't like what he saw. He became convinced that, except for one little girl with blue eyes and long, blonde curls, the Platt kids appeared to have Negro features. He told Mrs. Platt that parents of white students did not want her children in their school. He told her it was best to keep her children at home "until we can get this problem settled."

Mrs. Platt protested, explaining that they had descended from native Americans in the Carolinas, that they had birth and marriage certificates listing them as white and that her children had attended a white school in South Carolina prior to their arrival in Mount Dora.

"The sheriff remarked that he did not like Laura Belle's nose," Mrs. Platt later told investigators.

Angry and bewildered, the Platts kept their five children at home but Allen Platt decided to obtain documentation from the public school his children had attended in South Carolina.

In response, G.E. Brant, superintendent of schools in Orangeburg County, wrote a letter to Principal Roseborough at the Mount Dora school: "This is to certify that the children of Allen Platt have been attending the Crane Pond School, a white elementary school in the Holly Hill District of Orangeburg County, South Carolina. . ."

Brant went on to inform Roseborough, "I know Mr. Platt personally, and he is a fine fellow. His color is dark because of his Indian blood. I have checked with the oldest residents in Holly Hill, and they all say there is no Negro blood in the family."

But Principal Roseborough wouldn't be budged. He told Allen Platt that the matter was now in the hands of Sheriff McCall or the school board.

Platt appealed to the sheriff. McCall told him he was upholding state law which provided Negro and white schoolchildren with separate facilities. He told Platt to keep his children home unless he wanted trouble. He cited Article XII section 12 of the Florida Constitution, which said, that "White and Colored children shall not be taught in the same schools, but impartial provisions shall be made for both."

Under Florida law, the words "Negro," "Mulatto" and "Colored" were defined as applying to anyone who had one-eighth or more of African or Negro blood.

Further, McCall pointed out, Webster's Dictionary defined Croatan as "one of a people of mixed Indian, White and Negro blood living in North Carolina, now recognized as a distinct people."

All of this, of course, ignored the landmark U.S. Supreme Court ruling in May 1954 in the case of *Brown versus Board of Education of Topeka*. In it, the court declared: "Separate educational facilities are inherently unequal" and have no place in American public schools. It was certainly a significant ruling, but *Brown* would turn out to have little practical effect on the actual educational separation of the races in many public schools of that time. It was widely ignored, especially by "state's-righters" in the South.

The ensuing debates over state rights, state constitutions and state laws were to consume most of the public's attention, and the federal court ruling stood out like an unheeded beacon, giving the civil rights movement much of its purpose but having little immediate effect in the South, along with several other sections of the country.

In Lake County, the school board officially removed the names of the Platt children from the rolls of the Fifth Avenue School in Mount Dora and informed the parents they could enroll them in a Negro school.

The case attracted widespread attention, and debates erupted in newspapers and on the radio over the issue. Enjoying the fight, the sheriff was right in the middle of it.

CHAPTER 22

THE SEGREGATIONIST AND THE GOVERNOR

McCall announced to Lake Countians: "You may rest assured that I am opposed to integration in our schools and will use every legal means at my command to keep them on a segregated basis."

He ignored attacks from individuals and national publications for his "unilateral action" and outspoken views on the issue.

McCall questioned the marriage license for Allen and Laura Platt and the birth certificates of their children, which stated that they were considered white. McCall said he traveled to Columbia, South Carolina, to look at the state archives and found birth certificates which attested the Platts were part Negro.

The youngest child, blonde, blue-eyed Violet, had been adopted by the Platts, according to the records obtained by the sheriff.

Tempers flared in Lake County. There were a number of threats made that unless the Platts moved out of their Mount Dora neighborhood, there would be trouble. They would be "burned out" unless they packed up and left, one radio caller said.

Thus intimidated, the Platts moved to the little Orange

County town of Apopka, just a few miles down the road. Their attempts to enroll their children in a white school in Apopka also were blocked there, however.

Orange County School Superintendent Judson B. Walker said an investigation conducted by his office found discrepancies in the Platts' birth certificates and their account of having attended white schools in South Carolina.

Walker said he spoke to Superintendent Brant of the Holly Hill schools, who informed him the Platts had attended a special school classified as white and with white instructors but whose only students were Indian children. None of the Platts had attended white schools along with white children, Walker announced.

"The Platt children have not been denied an education," Walker said in Orlando. "They have a right to go to the Negro schools. Allowing them to go to white schools wouldn't work around here. It would be tragic if they tried to force their way into a school around here. You can't legislate feelings and prejudice out of peoples' minds."

The Platts appealed to the governor as a last resort.

"Mr. McCall is sheriff of Lake County and I am told it is dangerous in this country to antagonize him and that many law-abiding citizens are afraid of him," Allen Platt wrote in his letter to Gov. LeRoy Collins. "My experience with him shows this to be true. I am helpless under those conditions. I have no other recourse but to appeal to you to make a thorough investigation so that justice may be done. This I do."

The governor told reporters at the capitol: "He has made at least a *prima facie* case justifying an investigation and one will be made and made promptly."

Collins then took an unusual action.

After a quick look into the issue, the governor wrote Platt a long letter. He was sympathetic but pointed out the prevailing state law and urged that the Platts get the matter resolved through the courts by suing the Lake County School Board.

Although the board had stricken the Platt children's names from the student rolls at the Mount Dora school, Lake County School Superintendent C.A. Vaughn Jr. had left the door open, saying the issue was still under investigation and "if it is determined they do not have Negro blood, they are eligible to attend white schools."

Collins earned a reputation as one of Florida's most liberal-minded chief executives after years as a pacesetting legislator on civil rights issues — a highly unusual politician in deed as well as in his thinking. As governor from 1955 to 1961, Collins was widely admired by blacks, and excoriated by many whites, for urging peaceful acceptance of the Supreme Court's 1954 ruling on school desegregation.

In his lengthy letter to Platt, the governor spelled out the difficulties faced by Florida officials in enforcing the law on the one hand and attempting to exercise social justice on the other. There had long been controversy, he wrote, over whether Croatans have Negro blood. In short, there is no one answer under Florida law, the governor said, adding that the question can only be "properly resolved" through the court system.

The governor cautioned, however, that Platt's problem "goes much deeper than the law. You are getting a look at prejudice, perhaps the most tenacious and blinding of all the human emotions. Prejudice dethrones reason and justice and prospers in the atmosphere of fear which it spawns. . ."

Gov. Collins was being trying to be helpful, but he was careful in his advice to Platt.

"If you seek relief in our courts, I shall use the fullest power of the office I hold to enforce the final decree (of the court)," he wrote. "Further, I will urge the people in the area in which you are living to be tolerant of your ambitions for your children and cooperate fully in mind and spirit and deed to permit you and your family to enjoy fully your constitutional and lawful rights, whatever they may be declared to be. . ."

The governor continued in this vein in the lengthy letter, ending this way:

"Your children will not enhance their opportunities for the future in any school if they do not have peace of mind and the comfort of friends while getting an education. A legal victory alone would not assure these things. It is for you to decide, and I regret that I cannot be of greater assistance."

The turmoil unleashed by the issue soon came to be of a dimension equal to that of the Groveland Rape Case.

Sheriff McCall's actions had provoked a storm of criticism, particularly in northern newspapers and the weekly newsmagazines. He received numerous hate letters — from whites and blacks. Several threatened his life. On the other hand, some citizens, especially newcomers to the state, expressed outrage at the seeming insensitivity of many of the people in the region.

Mabel Reese, co-owner, reporter, columnist and editorial writer for the *Mount Dora Topic*, had turned against McCall since her arrival a few years earlier from the *Akron Beacon-Journal*. She had been one to praise him earlier for his actions in preventing a mob lynching, but now she lambasted the sheriff in her news columns and editorial pages as a hot-headed, simple-minded racist.

Mrs. Reese was a tenacious critic, who was praised by *Time Magazine* in its December 13, 1954, issue for spotlighting "the bullying sheriff," even at the cost of reprisals such as a flaming cross on her lawn, the poisoning of her dog and the smearing of "KKK" across her office windows.

News coverage such as this led to still another investigation by the U.S. Justice Department. U.S. Attorney James Guilmartin of Miami was assigned to head an FBI probe into any possible civil rights violations.

"We're not interested in the question of the children's education," Guilmartin said on arrival in Lake County. "The Supreme Court has not yet decided the segregation issue. All we're interested in is whether the civil rights of the Platts were violated by any peace officer."

"I haven't violated the civil rights of anyone or intimidated anyone," McCall said with a shrug, resigned to another investigation.

At about the time that he was pulling the Platt children out of school, McCall began promoting a movement called the National Association for the Advancement of White People (NAAWP). He was hoping it would compete for attention with the NAACP, because he blamed that black organization — in addition to "pink liberals" and Communist sympathizers — for trying to remove him from office.

The sheriff told the Leesburg Republican Women's Club that every woman should get a pistol "and learn how to use it. You have a perfect right under the federal Constitution."

He had begun a new role as a segregationist, even speaking at public forums, including a trip to Lincoln, Delaware, to speak at a rally of NAAWP members and supporters demonstrating against the integration of public schools in Milford and other Delaware towns.

This, of course, brought on a new wave of criticism against "the racist sheriff."

McCall calmly replied, "I have children in school and am going to do everything in my power to keep our schools on a segregated basis for them."

Although McCall denied years later that he was a racist, he didn't deny making statements like this: "I don't think there is any question about it, that the white race is superior to the black race. I believe that's a proven fact. In their native country, they're still eating each other. We don't do that."

He was a popular man with the voters in any case. He received more votes in the 1952 primary election than all three of his opponents combined. As a third-term elected official, he considered it his duty to speak up for what he and his supporters believed in. He received dozens of letters and notes of praise and encouragement for his tough stand.

At the time, McCall happened to be completing a two-year

term as president of the Florida Sheriffs Association, which ironically was holding its annual meeting in Eustis while the state and federal civil rights investigations into McCall's actions were taking place in neighboring Mount Dora.

"I don't think we have to apologize to other counties of Florida, and Florida doesn't have to apologize to other states for anything that has been going on," State Senator B. C. Pearce told the sheriffs convention. "We should tell the rest of the nation we stand for enforcing the things the Florida Constitution says we should enforce. I tip my hat to Willis McCall as one of the finest sheriffs who has ever served in the state of Florida."

In the meantime, a legal fund was helping the Platts bring their case to court, as the governor had suggested.

The family moved again, this time from Apopka to a little house by an orange grove near the town of Sorrento, on the county line between Lake and Orange counties. The children began receiving at-home tutoring from teachers of the Christian Home and Bible School, a white private school in Mount Dora.

The courts finally ruled on their case against the Lake County School Board.

Circuit Judge Futch surprised a lot of his friends and neighbors in October 1955 — a year after the Platt children had been forced out of school — by handing down a ruling permitting the Platts to enroll in any white public school in Florida.

Relying on the U.S. Supreme Court's *Brown vs. Board of Education* ruling in 1954, Futch declared the evidence "conclusively shows that the Platt children always attended white schools in South Carolina, belonged to white organizations, were fully recognized as white people in that state and are entitled to be so recognized here."

He surprised even more people by holding that a new law passed by the Florida Legislature earlier that year was a subterfuge "to circumvent the U.S. Supreme Court" to keep blacks out of Florida's white schools. The legislature had given county school boards the authority to assign students individually to schools in their districts.

The judge's ruling further stated that the act passed by state legislators "can serve no purpose except to further the practice of school boards in taking action and afterwards pretending to give consideration to what they had already done, as the Lake County School Board did in this case. This act is a farce, or rather a cover-up for farces, and can have no effect on the pleadings in this (Platt) case."

Surprisingly – for a Lake County jurist — Judge Futch was way ahead of the national trend. It wasn't until 1969 that the U.S. Supreme Court ordered public school districts to desegregate "at once."

CHAPTER 23

RULING'S AFTERMATH, FIREBOMBS AND FAMILY'S ORDEAL

Sheriff McCall immediately called Futch's ruling "disgraceful," among other choice words.

Ironically, one of the three lawyers representing the Platts was Jesse Hunter, the former county prosecutor who had been a close ally of the sheriff's and had now become a bitter foe.

Hunter did not run for reelection in 1952 and was now in private practice with his son Walton in an office across the street from the courthouse — and from McCall's jail and office — in Tavares. The two former friends had been feuding for several years. Hunter now rebuked the sheriff for criticizing the court ruling.

"Judge Futch is an honest man," Hunter said. "The attack on Judge Futch is outrageous."

The former state attorney branded "unfair" the publication of McCall's claims that the Platt family had Negro ancestry. Hunter said McCall didn't testify in court to that effect.

Asked about rumors that he had received threats, Hunter replied, "The only person who has threatened me has been Sheriff Willis McCall."

"Did he mean since Judge Futch's decision?"

"No, but plenty of times before," Hunter said without elaboration.

School board attorneys announced they would appeal the judge's ruling to the Florida Supreme Court.

Hunter then advised the Platt children not to enter a public school until the high court reviewed the case. Before they could go into a public school, however, the Christian Home and Bible School, which had provided tutoring for the children, decided to admit them fulltime. The five children were enrolled in the private school in November 1955.

The Platt home was firebombed that weekend.

Allen and Laura Platt and all of their seven children were watching television after 9 p.m. on a Friday night when they heard a loud noise in front of their house. Their dog began barking. Suddenly, an explosion of flames erupted on the back porch. Allen Platt and his son Denzell grabbed shotguns, jumped through the flames and fired at several running figures. But the attackers got into the nearby woods and made their escape.

The Platts fought the blaze with a water hose and finally succeeded in putting it out some twenty minutes later.

Called to the scene later that night, Sheriff McCall found seven or eight sets of footprints in the soft sand at the rear of the Platt house. He and his deputies found evidence indicating that two cars had been parked in a nearby orange grove, and they took plaster impressions of the footprints and tire marks.

"They might have been made by some high school boys who didn't want to go to school with burrheads," McCall said about the footprints.

But he also raised the possibility of "communistic elements."

"These leftwing elements have been stirring up this stuff . . . They don't care anything about the Platts. They just want to stir up a stink. . ."

A deputy state fire marshal called in from Orlando said after an inspection the following day that two one-gallon jugs of gasoline had been poured on the back porch and ignited.

Allen Platt told investigators that vehicles had been driving by his place for several days. Family members had seen white men near the house.

"I've always tried to treat people right, but if they try to bother me, I'll shoot," a harassed Platt told the sheriff and his deputies. "I just want to live in peace."

No blood was found at the scene. No arrests were made in the case.

As the Platts' lawyer, Hunter urgently asked Governor Collins for state protection for them. He urged action because the sheriff indicated he could not provide around-the-clock protection,

"It would be a great tragedy if this peaceful family is murdered and their home destroyed by fire," Hunter said.

"I'll be just as good to them as any other niggers I know of," McCall retorted. "I can't babysit with them. I can't go out there and live with them. If they (state officials) want to send someone down here, it's all right with me. I'll do as much as any other sheriff would do for any other family."

The governor took no action. But he told capitol reporters that the problems in troubled Lake County "have just got to stop. Not only are individual rights involved, but the good name and reputation of this fine county and our state have become involved."

McCall told me years later that he learned the governor had been about to suspend him, and even had a replacement in mind, except for the intervention of a few of his friends. He had been warned of the imminent suspension by another good friend, Dr. C.M. Tyre.

The sheriff said Dr. Tyre called him into his office and bluntly told him, "The governor wants to run you off, kick you out."

McCall quoted Dr. Tyre years later as telling him: "If you know anywhere to mend a fence, you'd better go do it. Collins has asked my brother Jim to take over as sheriff. . . He's not going to take the job, but he wants to give you a chance to do something."

McCall said he then got on the telephone with a number of influential friends.

"Five or six of them got to the governor and told him, 'You'd better lay off.' The next day, there was a press release saying the rumor was unfounded. The lying son of a bitch, he already had a man to replace me."

Dr. Tyre, his brother and the former governor weren't around to confirm McCall's story by the time he told it. But there is no evidence to indicate otherwise. McCall was on the verge of suspension several times in his career and later *was* suspended in another case by another governor.

Governor Collins was being pressured by the NAACP and other groups and individuals.

"Everytime I turned around they were investigatin' me," Mc-Call said later. "It was the Groveland thing, the Platt case, the labor organizers. They was gonna suspend me for malpractice. Under the law, I guess that's easy enough, you know."

As for the Platts, their house in Sorrento was peppered by a shotgun blast from a speeding car late one night in May 1956. An investigation showed buckshot splattered throughout the Platts' living room just a few feet from the bedroom where Allen and Laura Platt slept. No one was hurt.

The family was soon forced to move again, to another rural community in Orange County, where Allen Platt was employed at a woodworking shop. The five children continued to attend the Mount Dora Christian Home and Bible School.

With a slow, grudging acceptance of their status in the evolving era of school and social integration, the embattled Platt family eventually found a certain peace. Their names eventually faded from the headlines, and they finally left behind the controversy that had dogged their lives since they moved to Florida from their native South Carolina.

CHAPTER 24

FLAGS AND FOLDEROL

The sheriff was moving around comfortably now in his role as a segregationist, and he began expanding his interests well beyond his office. He made more public appearances and became more outspoken about his views.

He was a longtime member of the Benevolent and Protective Order of the Elks, and he now moved up in their hierarchy. He was an active member of the Kiwanis Club in Eustis, where he lived. He made speeches on Americanism and law enforcement to civics clubs and ladies' groups. He had two children in school and was an active member of the Parent-Teachers Association.

As a Lake County P-TA representative, McCall raised a fuss at a district meeting when he questioned the activities of the then-fledgling United Nations and some of its agencies, particularly the United Nations Educational, Scientific and Cultural Organization (UNESCO). He wanted the district organization to go on record as being opposed to UNESCO.

He pointed out that Julian Huxley, one of the original directors of UNESCO, and Bertrand Russell, one of its founders, considered the Christian religion "the principal enemy of moral progress in the world."

He was declared out of order by Delton Scudder, head of

the department of religion at the University of Florida, who told him, "If we pull out of UNESCO and continue to build bigger bombs, one of these days they are going to be dropped on us."

McCall replied tartly that "infiltration of Communism in our schools is far more dangerous than the dropping of bombs."

He was among a number of people who believed the United Nations was the first step toward a world government that would supplant our own national authority. Many were concerned about the Soviet Union's role in the UN and feared the world body would follow some of those principles, eroding the independence of Americans, making them subject to international law.

McCall became particularly incensed when the UN flag was raised above the Stars and Stripes at Arlington National Cemetery on United Nations Day in October 1950. President Truman had issued a proclamation celebrating the fifth anniversary of the UN, and the UN flag was displayed at many public functions throughout the country. Following that special observance, there had been a general movement to continue to fly the UN flag at all public buildings and to treat it on an equal basis with the American standard.

Part of the reason for this had to do with the Korean War, which was being fought under the UN banner, although the United States was furnishing most of the troops, armament and money for the multinational force.

Ultraconservatives such as McCall weren't buying the argument. They had a fear of Communism and linked the flag issue to the Cold War between the U.S. and the Soviet Union. The sheriff wanted to take make some kind of public statement, so he abruptly announced that he would not permit the UN flag to fly at the Lake County Courthouse alongside Old Glory.

The sheriff was following the example of Major General Sumter L. Lowry, commander of the 51st National Guard Division from Tampa, who introduced a protest resolution at a Guard convention in Washington. Gen. Lowry wanted President Truman to prohibit the display of the UN flag above or in an equal position to that of the U.S. banner.

"There is a conspiracy in this country to lower our own flag and put a world flag in its place," Lowry told the convention. Display of the UN flag above the American flag, such as was done at Arlington, "is an insult to every man who has ever given his life for the service of his country."

Sheriff McCall liked the crusty general's stand.

Lowry has "guts enough to defy the terrible influences that are creeping up from underground and eating away at the very fundamental principles of our so-cherished American way of freedom: the right of free speech and secret ballot and, above all, to worship our Almighty God as we see fit."

He fired off a letter to Governor Fuller Warren declaring himself "a red-blooded citizen of the old school" opposed to "a world federal form of government."

Alarmed by all of this, State Attorney Hunter decided to fight McCall.

The crafty, round-spectacled prosecutor saw the increasingly popular sheriff as a rival for political control of the county, and he was quick to anger when he thought the sheriff tried to exert too much authority. Hunter sent off telegrams to state and federal officials asking their views on displaying the two flags. He addressed the governor, Secretary of State Dean Acheson and General George C. Marshall, among others.

A week later, the county commission, following Hunter's advice, authorized the blue-and-silver symbol of the UN to fly next to the American flag in front of the courthouse. This was a direct rebuff to the sheriff.

"We see no objections and, in fact, we consider it our duty to fly the United Nations flag in front of the courthouse," said the commission's directive "We pledge allegiance to the United States government in its efforts through the United Nations to stop the spread of Communism and preserve the peace of the world."

Much to the sheriff's chagrin, the two banners soon fluttered

smartly in the cool November breeze from flagpoles of the same
height right in the center of his bailiwick.

But the sheriff had ignited great debate and heated discus-
sions in courthouse circles and public gathering places in and out
of Lake County. People took their patriotism seriously in these
parts. McCall was commended for his "courageous stand" by the
executive secretary of the National Society of the Daughters of
the American Revolution, Frances Barrett Lucas. The sheriff received scores of letters and telegrams in support.

The Florida Chamber of Commerce then declared it un-
American to fly the two flags at the same height. Echoing Lowry,
it called the practice "an insult to the men who have given their
lives in past wars."

Hunter replied in an open letter to the chamber published in
Sunday newspapers around the state. He accused the state business
organization of helping the Communist cause by failing to support
the UN at a time when the Soviets were saying the United States
was seeking to dominate the world body. He had no doubt, the
prosecutor added, that the chamber's resolution "has been cabled
to Joe Stalin and that he is very much pleased by it."

Glorying in the war of words he had created, Sheriff McCall
plopped his pointy-toed boots up on his desk and composed an
eloquent epistle of his own to the business group. It, too, received
much publicity. He called Hunter's arguments "learned but cir-
cuitous" and interpreted the law as saying that the American flag
"should take no back seat to any other flag."

The sheriff also demonstrated his protest of the county commission action by putting up a large American flag outside his
own office door on the first floor of the courthouse. The bottom
of the flag flapped in the face of anyone walking down the hall to
get to country offices from a building side door.

Outside the Lake County courthouse, the UN and U.S. banners snapped in the breeze on flagpoles of equal size.

The tall center pole in the middle of the two flags remained
bare.

CHAPTER 25

UNIONS, VIOLENCE AND COMMUNIST SPECTER

While Willis McCall was having the best time of his life as sheriff, there was one state official that couldn't turn around without
getting his day interrupted by the goings-on in Lake County: the
governor. Many a chief executive had lost sleep and had many a
meal or official function discombobulated when news arrived in
Tallahassee about McCall's latest adventures.

Gov. Collins and others warned him several times that he
couldn't engage in some of those free-ranging activities, but it
didn't seem to make much difference to McCall.

The controversies seemed to multiply when blacks were involved, individually or through the NAACP, or when some of the
trouble could be pinned on Communists. Sometimes, there was
a combination of the two elements, by McCall's calculation, and
he eagerly muscled right into the middle of anything like that.

He pointed out that the CIO labor group had been attacking him since 1948, when he squelched the activities of Axilrod and, in effect, ran him out of the state. After eleven years in
office, he told friends, the NAACP, the Communist Party, the
CIO, disgruntled politicians and others "have tried three times
to defeat me at the polls, have tried five times to have governors

remove me, have tried twice to have me indicted by federal grand juries."

One of McCall's bugaboos was the continuing effort to unionize farm and citrus workers.

Although the Food, Tobacco and Agricultural Workers union faded from the scene after the Axilrod case, other unions stepped up their activities in Florida. The CIO and the AFL (American Federation of Labor) vied with each other, sometimes violently, in their unionizing activities in the prosperous and growing citrus industry.

The United Packinghouse Workers (of the CIO) claimed it had recruited several thousand citrus pickers, truck drivers and other grove workers by the 1951-52 growing season. Growers and packinghouse owners contested the figures as inflated, claiming there was little interest by their employees in unions. They decried the violence they said was created by union activities.

One chilly October night in 1955, about a dozen citrus workers met with white UPW organizer James A. Luke at the Negro Masonic Lodge in the quiet little town of Umatilla. Ironically, this happened to be McCall's hometown.

The meeting was well under way when two shotgun blasts peppered the two-story wooden building, breaking windows and raining glass and pellets on those inside. Luke and the workers hit the floor. They could hear a speeding car in the darkness, but no one made an effort to leave. By the time they emerged, there was nothing to be seen.

At least two of the black workers were injured, one seriously enough to be hospitalized. He had shotgun pellets on his left side and arm but was not gravely hurt.

Union leaders then demanded that the governor suspend the sheriff on the grounds that he was unwilling to arrest those responsible, and that he condoned such actions.

McCall quickly counterattacked by calling the union organizers Communists. Then he packed up and left on a scheduled trip to South Florida with his wife Doris. They were celebrating their twenty-fifth wedding anniversary.

During the sheriff's investigation, the hospitalized man, Ardis Griffin, and other workers told deputies they saw a car full of white men cruising in the area of the lodge shortly before the shooting. The car was seen speeding away by neighborhood residents after the shotgun blasts.

UPW President Ralph Helstein cabled Sheriff McCall: "It is no accident that this brazen attempt to assassinate union leaders was made at a meeting of predominantly Negro workers and in a county in which your past record as sheriff has encouraged such terroristic attacks upon Negro citizens."

Governor Collins cabled the sheriff, sending a copy of the wire to Helstein, asking to be kept informed of the progress of the investigation and offering the services of the state in any way it could help. The shooting incident "must be fully investigated so that the guilty parties . . . will be brought to justice promptly."

McCall, who had returned to his office after his quick trip, wired back: "Rest assured that no efforts will be spared in finding guilty parties in Wednesday night shooting."

Several days later, the sheriff cabled the governor saying he would appreciate the assistance of the governor's investigator.

Luke, the white union official who had conducted the meeting, was tracked down by deputies in Polk County, adjoining Lake. He said he was reporting to his boss. He also had driven the injured man, Griffin, to a hospital in that county for treatment.

Luke told deputies he heard five shotgun blasts but never saw the men inside the speeding car. In a written statement, Luke said he didn't call police or the sheriff's office because the car had sped away.

"I think they were shooting to break up the meeting. I didn't see anybody with a hood on or a mask over their face. I was the first outside after the shooting, so if anybody saw anyone with their face covered, it had to be before the meeting started or somebody that was standing around on the outside or lived close by."

Luke later contradicted himself to reporters, saying, "We believe they were wearing white. They were wearing masks that covered their eyes like Lone Ranger masks. Their (car) license was covered with tape."

Luke's boss at the Packinghouse Workers union, Otis Nation, gave reporters an even more sensationalized account of the incident, which he did not witness. While Luke said there were 12 workers at the meeting, Nation said 23 Negro workers were present. He said a black Chrysler with four white men in it had been at the scene. When it stopped in front of the lodge, two men placed hoods over their heads and fired five blasts into the building through its two large windows on the ground floor.

Nation said there were 10 people injured.

Otis Nation, a white man who had a police record involving past union organizing efforts, blamed "hoodlumism" in Lake County for preventing an earlier union meeting. "Intimidating" leaflets were passed out by whites in Negro neighborhoods, he said, adding that he was warned he would be arrested if he came into the county.

He had been operating out of Winter Haven, in Polk County.

"McCall is unavailable at certain times when the law needs enforcing," the union leader said. But if Lake County workers want a union, "They're going to have it. Hitlerian tactics are not going to work."

Nation threatened to shut down the citrus industry if he found it necessary.

"We have organizations in every citrus county in Florida. And this season, we expect to have enough (members) to close the industry if the leaders are unwilling to sit down and bargain with us. We will naturally pick a time to strike when it will be the most-advantageous to us."

He refused to say how many workers belonged to the union

in Florida but estimated it would soon have the minimum of 10,000 needed to shut down harvesting operations. The tough talk surprised citrus industry executives and growers. Most of them scoffed at the union leader's claims and continued operations as usual, others were not so sure.

Workers were being enrolled in the UPW for an initiation fee of two dollars, with a membership fee of two dollars a month. This entitled them to strike benefits. Nation boasted of a UPW strike fund of more than $1.5 million.

On another front, the governor wired UPW President Helstein, rejecting a demand that McCall be suspended. The governor said "a diligent investigation" was being conducted. The sheriff had assured him of full protection for union-organizing meetings, Gov. Collins wrote Helstein.

That sure sounded like a vote of confidence for McCall.

However, the exasperated governor added a barbed little note that did not sit too well with the sheriff. The governor said he was "fully conscious of an unsatisfactory atmosphere surrounding law enforcement in Lake County and have assigned investigators from this office to that area."

This brought a quick rebuttal from McCall.

"The stink isn't coming from the law enforcement angle. The agitators have stirred it up — disgruntled politicians, the NAACP and the Communist Party. There isn't anything wrong with us," the sheriff said. "I think the governor may mean the people who have been attacking us."

He cooperated fully with the state investigator, however, and later wrote Collins a mollifying letter, outlining the investigative efforts and assuring him that everything possible was being done to turn up the guilty parties.

"I regret to say we have found absolutely no lead to work on," McCall wrote a week after the Masonic Lodge shooting. "Even though I feel that Otis Nation is a no-good Red agitator, I brand things of this nature deplorable and will do all in my power to keep such things from happening. I am sure if it were not for characters of this nature, such things would never happen."

Meanwhile, the sheriff publicized a sworn and notarized statement compiled by a detective agency on Otis Nation. It disclosed that the union leader had been arrested "several times in various parts of the United States, with three known convictions."

The most serious of these was a conviction and one-year sentence in California in 1947 for desertion from U.S. Army service. Others included a vagrancy charge in Oklahoma City in 1940 and violation of a state labor act for moving workers across the Florida border in 1943.

"I also have documents which connect him with the Communist Party and known Communist personnel on several occasions," along with reports from police departments in various cities "branding him a troublemaker," McCall's statement said.

The angry Nation — still keeping his distance in Polk County — admitted the convictions but denied he was a Communist. He denied his union was Communist-dominated, calling McCall's statements "typical McCarthy tactics," referring to Senator Joseph McCarthy's controversial investigations into Communist Party activities and membership in this country.

Nation said McCall threatened his life through his chief organizer, James Luke: "Tell Nation I am going to get him," the union leader quoted McCall. "He (Nation) is a Communist and the country would be better off without him. Tell him I said I was going to get him."

McCall called Luke a liar, and on and on it went. The governor refused to intervene directly. "There is no lawful basis for taking extraordinary executive action," he said.

Jesse Hunter, in his new role as a private attorney, journeyed to Tampa as a representative of citrus interests to talk with officials of the United Packinghouse Workers. He said he was concerned over strike threats and labor-recruiting activities.

"Such efforts only raise the race question," the former prosecutor said. "Pickers are now getting the best wages of any workers in the citrus industry. . . . A general strike would be an awfully serious thing."

This didn't stop Nation, who continued to direct organizing activities in Lake County from his headquarters in Polk County, which also was undergoing a great deal of union activity as the second-leading producer of citrus. He stepped up radio and leaflet attacks on state officials and agricultural leaders, plus attacks on the Florida State Employment Service and the Florida Fruit and Vegetable Association.

He said Florida was importing fruit harvesters from the Caribbean because growers didn't want to pay local workers living wages.

The CIO then abruptly stepped in and, in effect, stopped cold any more unionization of farmworkers and harvesters. Evidently feeling a lot of pressure from agriculture interests and newspaper editorial writers around the state, the CIO decided to disown Otis Nation and the United Packinghouse Workers union.

Howard D. Walton of Miami, the ranking CIO official in Florida announced that Nation had deviated from CIO policy and did not represent its official views.

Nation's actions and statements "have proved detrimental to the high standard of the CIO in Florida," said Walton, who was president of the Florida State Industrial Council of the CIO.

Nation "has been closely associated with several known Communists and their subsidiary organizations. His activities "have done much to deter the future organization and political activity of the CIO in Florida," said Walton.

"I wish to state firmly for the public and press that Otis Nation does not represent the views of the CIO as to methods of organizing workers, the use of Bahamian workers, the cooperative attitude and progressive methods of the Florida State Employment Service and the methods to be used in gaining fair treatment for that great mass of underprivileged and underpaid workers in the citrus and vegetable industry."

So, in effect, Walton was agreeing with Nation that workers were not fairly compensated, but he was totally opposed to Nation's methods.

It turned out that the UPW had never been officially affiliated with the Congress of Industrial Relations (CIO), Walton said.

"We don't have power to lift his charter or lift his paycheck, but we've been concerned with the bad publicity CIO has been getting and want people to know how we feel about this man. Nation can speak for UPW but not for CIO."

Nation retaliated. He said Walton was using the same information on his background obtained by Sheriff McCall.

"They keep saying these records are from FBI files. But these documents came from a private detective agency hired by people who have an interest in the Florida citrus industry for the purpose of smearing me and blackmailing me to keep me from organizing workers in Florida."

The head of the UPW told reporters he found it "strange that individuals in CIO, the industry and McCall would see eye-to-eye on something. All this smear and slander is not going to keep our workers from organizing and securing higher wages."

The outspoken union organizer threatened to "sue hell out of the whole bunch of them." But his credibility had been destroyed.

The UPW's activities among agriculture and citrus workers ground to a halt in Florida. And Otis Nation soon left the state under pressure from lawmen who were looking closely at some of the allegations raised by McCall and the CIO.

Once again, Sheriff's McCall's version of *lawandorder* had triumphed, this time over commies and union "agitators." His stock rose higher, particularly among the grateful citrus executives.

CHAPTER 26

WHITE RAPE SUSPECT

A strange case that seemed to have a never-ending conclusion for McCall and his deputies was one in which they and state lawyers were accused of railroading a mentally retarded *white* youth into a mental institution after a prominent white matron reported she had been raped in her home by a *black* man.

That one cost the state $75,000 in compensation after the intervention of the governor, plus state and federal investigations conducted many years after the crime.

The woman, a resident of the village of Okahumpka, sounded the alarm early on a dark, cool December morning with a call to the sheriff's office. When deputies descended on the big, two-story house, she said an intruder had assaulted her in her bed while her husband was away. She was hysterical but told the officers her attacker was a black man.

The lawmen quickly began rounding up suspects in the Negro community and hauling them in for questioning. The total reached 22 over the next few days.

Evidence turned up at the scene included a pair of undershorts evidently worn by the rapist and a diamond-shaped heel print on the ground outside the house. McCall said a few days later he had a firm suspect, a black man, who fit the victim's description and whose shoes matched the heel print.

A few days later, the NAACP protested that the black youth was being held incommunicado and had not been formally charged. Concerned, Governor Collins queried the state attorney in Lake, at the time Gordon Oldham Jr., who assured the governor the suspect had now been allowed to see his grandparents, who were in the process of obtaining a lawyer.

Ten days went by before the sheriff and prosecutor made a surprise announcement: a 19-year-old *white* youth had been arrested and had confessed to the rape. There was no immediate word on the black suspect.

Jesse Daniels, the white youth, was a bright, handsome, easy-going youngster before he was stricken with rheumatic fever and came close to death at the age of eight. That and two subsequent attacks left him mentally retarded. His poor parents tried, on and off, to place him in a state-run farm for handicapped children in Gainesville, but they were repeatedly turned down for lack of room. They couldn't afford any other type of care.

Jesse grew into a thin, gangly youth, quiet and outwardly normal, sheltered at their modest Okahumpka home by his doting parents: Charles Daniels, now ailing and nearly 70, and his wife Pearl, who was in her 40s.

Five days after the rape and two days before Christmas, a deputy showed up at the Daniels' house and politely told them he wanted to take Jesse into Tavares to "ask him a few questions." The parents were alarmed, but they were assured he would be brought back soon.

Jesse didn't come home that night, however, and the worried Danielses drove to the Tavares jail early the following morning. There, they were told by prosecutor Oldham that their son was in jail and that the sheriff wanted to hold him a while longer for questioning. The Danielses went home.

They heard no more until four days later, when Oldham and the sheriff publicly announced that Jesse had confessed to the crime. McCall called on Charles and Pearl Daniels personally to inform them about the case against their son.

Mr. and Mrs. Daniels had questions.

What about the victim's statement that she had been raped by a black man? What of the diamond-shaped heel print and the shorts found at the scene? What happened to the Negro suspect? Why had Jesse been held so long without being allowed to see his parents or a lawyer? Was he competent enough to sign a confession?

McCall replied that the victim must have been confused about her assailant because the attack took place in the dark. She was "hysterical and not rational. She thought it *might* have been a black man, but she wasn't sure until we talked to her a few days later."

McCall later explained that the Negro suspect evidently had walked through the victim's backyard a day or two earlier because his shoes matched the diamond-shaped heel print. But the young black was released after Jesse's confession.

When the American Civil Liberties Union tried to intervene in Jesse's case, the sheriff told one of the ACLU lawyers he was not needed or wanted since the family had told him that if their son needed an attorney, they would get one they knew.

The shorts found at the scene were reported to be Jesse's. Deputies compared them to underwear taken off the clothesline at the Daniels home. Deputies said the youth even knew the color of the carpeting on the staircase of the victim's home (maroon). And they said he described the furniture in the victim's bedroom.

"My deputies found other footprints outside the (victim's) house and tracked them to Jesse's house," the sheriff said. "They found that his shoes matched tracks found in the yard. . . He had undressed downstairs before he went up to that bedroom and left his underwear. . . He described the wooden front door to the house, saying, 'it was tight like it had got wet and swelled.'

"He described the house too well to have made it up."

The parents protested, to the sheriff, to the prosecutor, to the governor.

In a three-page handwritten letter to Governor Collins, Mrs. Daniels wrote that she believed her son had been "brainwashed" into confessing the crime. She wrote:

"After obtaining the confession, McCall did allow us one minute, under guard, to see the boy on Saturday and when I kissed the pitiful child saying we love, trusted and believed in him, McCall grabbed my arm and jerked me off balance, telling me not to ever ask to see the boy again – that 'you will never see him again.'

"Am I supposed to be man-handled by him? What law is that, Sir?"

The governor called on the sheriff and prosecutor for an explanation. The sheriff said the woman had broken her word not to discuss the case with her son.

"The mother kept saying, 'Jesse, you know you didn't do it. Tell them you didn't do it.'"

The Danielses decided to appeal to the public through reporters. They said their son never left the house the night of the crime. He slept in the same bedroom with his father and could not have sneaked out and back in without the father awakening because the elder Daniels slept lightly due to a heart ailment.

But the teenager's confession led to a grand jury indictment.

Judge Futch appointed an attorney for young Daniels after finding that the parents were indigent. The elderly father was a disabled World War I veteran with a heart condition, and the family lived in a small house.

The judge then directed that Jesse be sent to the state mental hospital in Chattahoochee, in Florida's Panhandle, for a determination as to whether he was competent to stand trial. Two psychiatrists there determined that he was "mentally incompetent."

The psychiatric report spoke of the teenager's lack of education and the fact that he slept with a teddy bear. However, the psychiatrists said, the confession did, indeed, appear to be Jesse's.

Their decision was based on the detail the young man provided of the victim's house and the circumstances of the crime. The "descriptive account" Jesse gave of his behavior the night of the assault "indicates that he had performed the act with which he is charged."

Judge Futch had Jesse returned to court for a hearing, formally declared him incompetent to stand trial and committed him to the mental hospital. Under Florida law, he was to remain there until he was mentally competent to undergo a trial, if ever.

Criticism was heaped on the heads of the sheriff, the prosecutor, the judge and the court-appointed attorney who had agreed to the judge's finding. Jesse Daniels was railroaded into an insane asylum, the critics said. Some of them even said county law enforcement officials were pressured to forget about a Negro since it would somehow be more acceptable for a well-to-do white woman to have been raped by a white man than a black, especially in her own home.

Surprisingly, McCall ignored the criticism, as did the others.

Meanwhile, there were a number of other break-ins, two attempted rapes and reports of a peeping-tom in the same Okahumpka-Leesburg area.

A young housewife who lived near the Daniels house was awakened in the middle of the night to find a man standing by her bed. Her screams woke up her husband and sent the intruder dashing out of the dark bedroom. She could not provide an adequate description of the man and no follow-up clues were found by deputies.

Police and deputies answered a number of similar calls for weeks.

In April, 1958, a 62-year-old white woman was raped in the Leesburg home of her employers, a handicapped woman and her brother, for whom she kept house. A Leesburg patrolman called to the scene spotted a man running in an orange grove near the house. The officer fired his shotgun and the man fell.

Advancing cautiously, the policeman saw the man rise up and start to run off. He fired a second time. The man fell and screamed, "Oh, Lord, you hit me. Please don't shoot me again." As the officer approached, the wounded man cried out, "I did not rape the woman."

Eighteen-year-old Wiley Sam Odom, a lanky Negro who lived in Okahumpka, confessed to the rape to Leesburg Police Chief W.L. Fisher and Sheriff McCall.

The following month, in what was believed a record time for a capital case, an all-white male jury found Odom guilty of rape. The trial began at 3 o'clock in the afternoon and was over by 8 o'clock that night. The jury deliberated eight minutes.

Judge Futch quickly sentenced Odom to the electric chair.

Chief Fisher said that with Odom's arrest, the series of break-ins, burglaries and attempted rapes dating from the previous November had come to an end.

The Danielses and others contended that Odom had also been the guilty party in the Okahumpka rape of the white woman in December. But nothing came of their protests that Jesse Daniels had been innocent when he was committed to the mental hospital.

More than a year later, in August 1959, shortly before his execution, Wiley Odom admitted to raping the elderly woman in Leesurg because he had been "drinking wine and 'shine, and it was the 'shine that told me to do it."

Odom then made a startling admission to reporter Mabel Reese of Lake County: He said he knew the man who had raped the well-to-do Okahumpka woman around Christmastime 1958, and it wasn't Jesse Daniels.

The reporter quoted Odom as saying, "I didn't do it, but I'll confess if you want me to. Sure won't hurt me any now."

But Odom was put to death in Ol' Sparky, Florida's electric chair, on August 29, 1959, after telling State Attorney Gordon

Oldham he had made the statement about Daniels in an effort to put off his execution.

The Daniels case lay dormant for more than 10 years. Jesse's father died shortly after his son's commitment, but his mother continued her efforts to free him. In 1971, a staff committee of six doctors at the Chattahoochee institution – at the urging of attorneys – recommended that he be released from custody.

A court-appointed lawyer brought the case before the circuit court in Lake County, asking that Daniels be declared sane so he could face the rape charge. But Judge E. R. Mills Jr. ruled that he was still incompetent to stand trial.

An appeals court overruled the finding, and it also ordered the defendant to be released pending any trial.

Jesse Daniels was freed on December 4, 1971, almost 14 years after the crime. He was now 33 years old.

"It's the happiest day of my life, the best day I've ever had,' he said upon arriving at his mother's house. She had moved to Daytona Beach after remarrying.

He was still slender, softspoken and slow-moving, almost boyish in appearance. He said he hadn't raped the woman, that he confessed to it because he was afraid of Sheriff McCall: "He told me he would kill me if I didn't sign the confession saying I was guilty."

The surprisingly articulate Daniels spent most of the first few weeks at home, strumming his guitar and ruminating with reporters and family friends over his time in the institution.

"To be locked up all those years was pure torture," he said. "I thought to myself I would never get out, that I was put there for the rest of my life. I'm bitter. It's hard to forgive what's happened. It cost me 14 years and destroyed my teenage life."

McCall angrily denied any wrongdoing. He pointed out that he was just one of many officials involved in the case which resulted in Daniels' commitment.

The state formally dropped the 14-year-old rape charge after the state attorney's office decided it would be impossible to bring all the elements of the case together again for a retrial.

A year later, a federal grand jury was convened in Jacksonville to determine whether Daniels' civil rights had been violated. It heard from Daniels and several of McCall's investigators, but the sheriff was not called. The grand jury returned no indictments and adjourned in August 1973.

"I knew all the time they would not get an indictment," the sheriff said. "This has been a political harassment thing from the word go."

The Florida House of Representatives' Committee on Retirement, Personnel and Claims then got into the act. It decided to look into the case to determine whether the state had any liability. Investigator Thomas Woods said in his report he uncovered evidence that indicated the Okahumpka rape was committed by Sam Wiley Odom.

Statements made by Odom while awaiting execution for the separate rape case contained details of the Okahumpka case which only the actual rapist would have known, according to Woods.

In 1974, the Florida Legislature awarded Jesse Daniels $75,000 as compensation. It rejected a bill that would have awarded $25,000 to Mrs. Daniels.

CHAPTER 27

FAKED FOOTPRINTS, WHISTLEBLOWERS AND SUCH

Yet another inflammatory rape case brought accusations against some of McCall's men that they had manufactured evidence used to send two blacks to the death house. The violent attack put the woman into a mental institution, and the case brought about a complex maze of rulings from state and federal investigators and judges over the next fifteen years.

Perhaps the strangest thing about it, however, was that the whistleblowers against two sheriff's deputies were two of McCall's former deputies.

The case developed slowly, gathered steam and subsequently resulted in headline-making allegations on both sides. McCall, as usual, was right in the middle of it. But with a difference. He was defending his men along with his own effectiveness in upholding *lawandorder*.

Shortly after midnight on a cool night in March, 1960, a 56-year-old spinster who lived alone in the community of Fruitland Park staggered to a neighbor's house about a half-mile away and collapsed in a pool of blood.

Local police were called and she was transported to a hospital, where doctors discovered she had been raped, kicked and beaten. Her sexual organs were torn and bleeding. Her attackers had split her skull open with a steel bar or, possibly, a hammer. Her ribs were fractured and some of her teeth were sticking through her cheeks.

Sheriff's deputies who went to her house found it had been ransacked.

Using bloodhounds early the next morning, deputies followed tracks leading away from the victim's rural home through the woods and gullies up to another house about half a mile away. There, the officers awakened and arrested two men for investigation of breaking and entering and assault. A third man was arrested at a movie theater in Leesburg that night.

Deputies found shoeprints in the sand and clay outside the victim's house and made plaster casts of six of them. When the suspects' shoes were compared to the plaster casts from the scene, they didn't match.

Under questioning, however, one of the suspects admitted to helping plan a robbery at the woman's house. He told deputies he had been at the scene that night with two others men but had not taken part in the break-in and rape. Significantly, he also said all three had purposely worn old shoes to disguise any tracks and that they had dumped them after the break-in at a clay pit on the road between Fruitland Park and Montclair.

After a search, the discarded shoes were found and compared to the plaster casts. One-by-one, the deputies found that they matched.

Two of the men under arrest, Jerry Chatman and Robert Shuler, were charged with rape, a capital offense calling for the death penalty. They signed confessions. The third suspect, Levi Summers, had talked and directed deputies to the clay pit where the shoes were found.

The attending physician, Dr. George Engelhard, found the rape victim "badly bruised, battered, lacerated and befuddled."

Assistant State Attorney John W. McCormick saw her at the hospital about twelve hours after she was admitted and had a difficult time questioning her. He described her as incoherent.

An investigator for the Florida Sheriff's Bureau came to the hospital the following day and said, "She really did not know too much what had occurred except she remembered some individuals being at her home. She just didn't know."

After the victim remained in that mental condition for some time, Dr. Engelhard determined her to be incompetent and signed the necessary paperwork for her commitment — along with the county court — to a mental institution.

At trial, Summers testified he had accompanied his buddies to the isolated house and helped the friends break in. But he said he never went inside, that he waited outside in the dark. When his friends rejoined him about a half-hour later, Summers told the jury, they told him they "had to kill her."

Summers then testified about the old shoes, how the men disposed of them.

The rape victim was by then in a mental institution and was not called to testify. A long, rambling, confused statement obtained from her by the prosecution was not introduced at trial.

The prosecution did present a pair of bloody shorts and a bloody handkerchief that were marked as coming from Shuler. The most damaging evidence, however, seemed to be the plaster casts that matched the discarded shoes belonging to the defendants.

Chatman and Shuler did not testify. They were convicted and sentenced to death. Because of his cooperation and testimony, Summers was discharged by the court.

The Florida Supreme Court affirmed the convictions and sentences on direct appeal. About a year after trial, the two convicts filed handwritten appeals, alleging that their confessions had been forced and that they had been tricked and threatened. Florida's high court denied their petitions without comment.

In September 1962, their Tampa attorney, Francisco Rodriguez, filed a writ of habeas corpus for the death row inmates with the Florida court. It called for a new trial. The claim was based, in part, on a statement made by former Lake County deputies Thomas L. Ledford and Noel E. Griffin Jr.

Ledford and Griffin claimed they had overheard Deputy Lucius G. Clark say that he and Deputy James L. Yates had poured the plaster impressions of the shoeprints in Clark's backyard, rather than at the rape scene. The petition to the state Supreme Court alleged that Chatman and Shuler had thus been convicted with faked shoeprints.

The petition asked the court to determine whether there had been a conspiracy involving deputies Yates and Clark and Sheriff McCall and State Attorney Gordon Oldham to convict the defendants by falsifying evidence and suppressing information available to them.

The high court granted a stay of execution until a hearing could be held.

Ledford and Griffin had been fired by the sheriff, on separate occasions, in early 1962. They made their allegations of false evidence about three months later.

Griffin said he lost his job because he had informed the sheriff that one of his other deputies was taking kickbacks from a supplier of moonshine. Asked about this, McCall denied it, saying he fired Griffin because he had been charged with killing hogs at a ranch in Volusia County. "I arrested him and fired him on the spot," the sheriff said.

Ledford also was charged in the hog-killing case. But he had been fired as a deputy before that incident because, according to McCall, Ledford had demonstrated "overbearing tactics" on several occasions.

Ledford, Griffin and three hunting companions had appeared before a Volusia County judge after the ranchowners complained that their hogs had been slaughtered. The hunters claimed the hogs were wild. Before trial, the judge dismissed the case at the request of the prosecution. The ranchers could not prove the hogs were theirs, the prosecutor said, and they had decided to drop the charges.

Sheriff McCall asserted that Ledford and Griffin were now making their accusations of manufactured evidence out of spite, to get even with him and deputies Yates and Clark, whom they disliked.

Disregarding this, Circuit Judge Troy Hall, a bitter political foe of the sheriff's, asked a grand jury in Orlando to investigate the allegations.

In December 1962, the grand jury indicted the deputies, Clark and Yates, on charges of conspiracy to commit perjury. In addition, Yates was charged with perjury. The panel said Yates had falsely sworn and identified the footprint casts as having been made at the crime scene. And, the jury said, Yates and Clark had plotted together to lie about the evidence.

FBI agents testified that lab tests showed that dirt on the shoeprint casts matched the soil of Clark's backyard and was not similar to that from the area around the victim's home.

While the Orlando grand jury was working on the case, the Florida high court also appointed a special commissioner to study the record and hold a hearing to determine whether convicts Chatman and Shuler should be granted a new trial.

The special commissioner, retired judge L.L. Parks, reported to the court in May 1963 that the former deputies' testimony before the grand jury "was not worthy of belief." Parks said the testimony presented by ex-deputies Yates and Clark was not consistent with the allegations made in their original statement, and the unusual delay in making their claims against Ledford and Griffin "raises grave doubt as to their motives, then or now."

He discounted the FBI crime lab reports on soil samples because they had not been made until 18 months after the crime.

Parks determined, however, that he could not legally conclude that "the casts in question were in fact falsified." The state Supreme Court then denied the motion for a new trial for the death row convicts.

Later, Circuit Judge Carrroll W. Fussell threw out the indictments of the former deputies, Clark and Yates, citing a two-year statute of limitations on the perjury charges. They were not prosecuted.

In May 1964, the prisoners again appealed, this time to the federal district court in Jacksonville. This court did not issue a ruling until *eight* years later. In May 1972, U.S. District Judge Charles R. Scott ruled in the convicts' favor, agreeing with their principal argument that the footprint plaster casts were faked.

Scott also agreed that the victim's rambling statement should have been voluntarily supplied by the prosecution to the defense. Further, the judge said, the bloody shorts and bloody handkerchief introduced as evidence at trial were obtained as a result of an unlawful search and seizure of Shuler's rented room.

Judge Scott ordered a new trial.

Almost 12 years after they were convicted, the prisoners were removed from death row and placed in the general prison population.

"There's no doubt in my mind that they were guilty," said the angry sheriff after the appeals court ruling.

The state then stepped back in and appealed Judge Scott's ruling to the U.S. Fifth Circuit Court of Appeals in New Orlando.

Two years later, the court overruled Scott on the allegedly faked footprints and the claim that the prosecution had suppressed the victim's statement. It also said the question of unlawful search-and-seizure was an issue to be decided by a state court.

The tribunal criticized the lower federal-court's judge for not fully considering the arguments of prosecutor Oldham, Sheriff McCall, and deputies Yates and Clark, who contended that that the plaster casts had been properly made at the scene of the crime.

The complaining former deputies had argued that there were only three partial footprints at the victim's house, that it had rained that day and that chickens running around, plus deep sand around the house made prints impossible.

The federal appeals court said the lower federal court in Jacksonville accepted as fact, not opinion, the FBI testimony that the soil on the plaster casts matched that from Clark's yard and not that of the victim's property. The court in New Orleans quoted Assistant State Attorney McCormick, from the trial record, to the effect that there were tracks underneath the window and in the yard. It said McCormick saw the casts being made and that he was at the jail when some of the defendants' shoes were brought in.

It quoted from testimony by the sheriff: "You could tell where they walked all over the yard. . . There were plenty of good tracks."

The court then concluded that the Ledford-Griffith testimony was "overwhelmingly refuted" by the testimony of others.

So . . . Chatman and Shuler were right back where they started.

During the lengthy appeals, however, a U.S. Supreme Court decision abolished the death penalty and lower courts were required to resentence all convicts awaiting execution.

In March 1975, Chatman and Shuler came before Judge Hall in Tavares. They had been in prison almost 15 years, 12 of them just a few steps away from Florida's three-legged electric chair called "Ol' Sparky" by all.

Now, they had a not-surprising request: They asked for their freedom.

Addressing the court, Chatman asked the judge to consider his and Shuler's good records during their prison time. In support of their cause were letters from the rape victim, now 71-one years old. She had been discharged from the mental facility several years earlier and gone to live out of state.

"It is agreeable with me that you (release) the men mentioned," Judge Hall quoted part of her letter in court. Her brother also endorsed the request in a letter saying the prisoners "have both spent more time than they should have. I say they should be made free again."

The judge found the requests "most unusual" and said he didn't think it within his province to grant them. He did the next best thing, however. He resentenced Chatman and Shuler to forty years in prison.

This made them eligible for parole, which they eventually were granted.

Chapter 28

Jailhouse Beating and Death

Having gained a reputation as a strict segregationist (many called him a redneck racist), McCall became involved in a series of cases in the 1950s and '60s in which the investigative tactics used by him and his deputies were so egregious that some of the black men often languished in jail for months with or without having had trials.

Being black and being suspected of rape in Lake County was dangerous to your health and well being.

A number of these episodes again involved state and federal civil rights investigations, but McCall was always cleared of wrongdoing.

There was one case, however, in which the situation got completely out of control. And McCall eventually paid for it dearly. Surprisingly, the whole thing started because of a traffic ticket. It wasn't a capital crime case in the beginning, but McCall made it one. And he came to regret it. It caused him more serious problems than even the Groveland Rape Case did.

It was the fatal beating of a prisoner in his jail cell.

Tommy J. Vickers, a mentally troubled black man from Miami, had his first encounter with the law in Lake County on Sept. 5,

1971. While driving north to visit his dying mother in Georgia, his car was stopped by a Florida Highway Patrol trooper. He was ticketed for an expired safety inspection sticker on his auto windshield.

Because he failed to post a $26-dollar bond or answer a court summons, Vickers was eventually returned from Miami to Lake County in handcuffs.

Vickers was 37, of average build, but strong. He had a history of mental illness dating back to a motorcycle accident in the Bahamas in 1967. He had been in and out of scrapes with the law in Miami since then. He was divorced and the father of two children.

In April 1969, he was admitted to the psychiatric ward at Jackson Memorial Hospital in Miami suffering from an acute schizophrenic episode. He was released two-and-a-half months later. On April 6, 1972, he was arrested for disorderly conduct and again wound up in the psychiatric ward at Jackson. This time, he was found to be physically and mentally sound and was turned over to the Dade County jail.

Jailers reported strange behavior and Vickers was again transferred to the hospital for observation. He was then released. A couple of days after that, officers responded to another call concerning Vickers and arrested him. It was during that incarceration that a Lake County bench warrant for his arrest came to light.

Officials in Lake County were notified, and a judge signed an order to return Vickers to Tavares for prosecution on the traffic ticket and his failure to answer repeated summonses from the court. Dade County police warned Lake County deputies of his mental difficulties and reported that he was occasionally violent.

Vickers was driven the 300 miles from Miami to Lake County without incident. He was handcuffed and shackled. Upon his arrival at the jail, a report entered by deputy Elbert Foster, who brought him in, noted that Vickers was a "Signal 20" (a possible mental case).

He was placed in Cell 2C of the Lake County jail on April 12, 1972. The trouble began a few hours later.

Vickers began beating and kicking on the door and walls of his cell, and he was transferred to a "tile cell." This was a small, padded cell with cheap tile floors containing only a mattress and used for prisoners who could hurt themselves. On and off through the night, the prisoner beat a tattoo on the cell door, creating a terrible disturbance in the generally orderly jail, which had been recently rebuilt into a modern facility that could hold up to 200 inmates.

The following day, Sheriff McCall, several deputies and trusties attempted to quiet Vickers, who was once again yelling and throwing food around in his cell. There was an altercation with those who entered the cell. The prisoner was eventually subdued and placed in a "Ceech tank," a six-by-six-foot box with thin, spring-backed, stainless steel walls, floor and ceiling. The tank, which had no toilet facilities or furniture of any kind, was designed for violent prisoners.

On April 14, McCall petitioned the county court, formally requesting a mental examination of Vickers. But the prisoner stayed in jail, primarily in the Creech tank, until April 20, when he was transferred to Waterman Memorial Hospital in Eustis.

He was in bad shape on arrival, both physically and mentally. He complained of pain in his side. He died in the hospital three days later.

McCall was on vacation in Hawaii.

A six-man coroner's inquest jury was convened.

Several jail inmates testified that Vickers was beaten on several occasions, but trusties and jailers denied it. Deputies, ambulance attendants and a doctor testified Vickers was violent and uncontrollable at times. Personnel at Waterman Hospital said he was unmanageable and bit one attendant while they were attempting to subdue him.

Aside from his mental state, a hospital physician had made

a tentative diagnosis that Vickers suffered a kidney ailment. He was undergoing treatment when he died.

Dr. William H. Shutze, who conducted the required autopsy, testified that Vickers suffered peritonitis (acute inflammation of the stomach lining) resulting from a blow between four days and two weeks prior to death. This covered the time period he was in jail in Dade and Lake counties, and in the hospital.

On May 12, the coroner's jury ruled that the cause of death was due to "acute peritonitis as a result of a blow to the lower abdomen incurred by mischance or accident, said blow inflicted by person or persons unknown."

Presiding Judge L.R. Husstetler Jr. explained that the verdict "essentially means he was mistreated somewhere . . . but that the jury had no testimony to point to anyone."

McCall, who returned to Tavares following the prisoner's death, said the prisoner "had to be subdued all along the line. There is no telling where or how he got the injury. To my knowledge, he was not mistreated here."

But to persistent questions, the garrulous McCall freely admitted to reporters that he had "popped" Vickers on the back of the head. "When he tried to attack me, I popped him on the back of the head with my open hand," he said. The blow "calmed" Vickers.

A week later, Gov. Reubin Askew ordered an investigation into the suspicious death. The governor sent in officials from the state's investigative agency, the Florida Department of Law Enforcement, to assist Gordon Oldham, the state attorney in Lake County.

A few days later, the governor sent his general counsel, Edgar M. Dunn Jr., before Judge Troy Hall in Tavares to request that a fullscale grand jury investigation be conducted by a panel chosen from outside Lake County. And he wanted an outside prosecutor.

Askew's reasoning was that Sheriff McCall could be "a principal suspect" in Vickers' death.

"Conditions in Lake County make it impractical to convene a grand jury in said county," said the governor's petition to the court. "It appears . . . that the sheriff of Lake County and one or more of his deputy sheriffs or jailer may be material witnesses or even the principal suspects in connection with the said grand jury investigation."

Judge Hall agreed with the governor's petition. It probably helped that he had been a political enemy of the sheriff's for more than a decade. The judge also granted a request from Askew to remove from the sheriff's custody ten inmates who had been at the jail at the same time as Vickers. Some of them had testified at the inquest.

Gov. Askew contended that it was necessary to transfer the inmates to another jail to protect them "against reprisals and potential threats" as well as to make them available to a grand jury. Askew then appointed State Attorney Robert Egan of neighboring Orange County as special investigator. The grand jury was to be convened in Orlando, the county seat.

"Well, this is typical. It happens every time there is an election year," McCall groused to friends. "I have always believed that if you can't stand the heat, you ought to get out of the kitchen. And I'm not ready to quit cooking yet."

At the same time, a federal judge had overturned the convictions of two blacks who had been sentenced to death 12 years earlier on a rape case in Lake County. State investigators also were looking into that case, and McCall's role in it, along with that of State Attorney Oldham. Oldham was alleged to have conspired with others in presenting falsified evidence to the jury.

The "old boy" situation in Lake County was really getting out of hand.

CHAPTER 29

SHERIFF'S MURDER INDICTMENT

McCall sat down and did some serious thinking. He determined that his career hung in the balance with the Vickers case because of the outside prosecutor and its venue change to Orlando, where members of a grand jury might not be as sympathetic to the way things were done in Lake County.

He tried to keep the proceedings in Tavares, arguing that the transfer was illegal. And he had a lot of people agreeing with him.

The sheriff also filed an affidavit of prejudice against Judge Hall, who transferred the official investigation to Orlando. McCall charged him with "animosity, hostility and personal conflict" toward him over a period of many years. The judge, "on many occasions, uttered derogatory remarks" about him and had attempted "by surreptitious and other means" to have him removed from office.

Some Lake Countians were not at all happy with "Mr. Askew" (said derogatorily) for stepping into their bailiwick. Florida and federal officials had been poking their noses into their affairs for far too long, they believed.

Bob Barth, a Eustis shopowner, said, "I've had just about enough of this federal-state interference like this. Lake County people elected this sheriff and if they are going to investigate him, it ought to be done by Lake County people."

Said Leesburg Mayor Sam Pyles, "I think we have law and order in Lake County the same or more than in Orange County."

Eustis businessman Clayton Bishop didn't think the governor "has enough intelligence to know what is going on. I think we ought to convene a grand jury to investigate the governor."

Initially, even Florida Attorney General Bob Shevin expressed misgivings about having a grand jury in one county investigate the actions of officials in another.

"My gut reaction is that it is probably not legal," Shevin said. "The point is, would an Orange County grand jury have any authority to indict, assuming there was a crime committed, a Lake County law enforcement officer or anyone else for a crime that was committed in Lake County?"

But State Attorney Bob Eagan in Orange County went right on with his investigation while everybody was debating the issue.

On the night before the grand jury met in Orlando, the sheriff made an appearance on an Orlando television station. On a program called "Central Florida Showcase," McCall blamed Communists, militant black groups and Judge Troy Hall for his troubles. He accused Hall of trying to become a political boss in the county.

"Judge Hall doesn't like me. He doesn't come right out and tell you to your face — he does it behind your back. He's a backstabber."

In his answers to three interviewers on the TV program, McCall said it was apparent to him that Vickers was mentally disturbed. Although he was being held in an isolation cell, "He belonged in a maximum security mental ward. He was tossing his food around and yelling."

The sheriff said he sent two men into the cell to quiet Vickers and the prisoner had become violent, grabbing the guards and crashing to the floor of the cell with them all in a tangle.

"He broke loose from them and came at me. I popped him a couple of times. So far as I know, I was the only one to touch him."

No blackjack or weapon was used, the sheriff said. He had used only his hands.

"I don't know who hit him in the stomach. I don't know what caused him to die. I don't know if his death was due to a stomach blow."

Smiling and relaxed, McCall appeared before a 23-member grand jury in Orlando the following day. He waived immunity from prosecution, meaning that anything he said could be used against him.

Conducting its inquiry behind closed doors, the panel spent less than a week hearing testimony from some 40 witnesses, including 11 prisoners and several deputies from the Lake County jail.

On the following Monday, June 12, 1972, Sheriff Willis V. McCall was indicted on charges of second-degree murder, aggravated battery and aggravated assault. The grand jury decided that McCall demonstrated "a depraved mind" while kicking inmate Vickers to death.

Recalling the bitter process, McCall told me years later that an FDLE agent called his office in Tavares immediately after the indictment was handed down. "He (the agent) had my radio operator crying by telling her I was no longer sheriff." The agent went on to tell the woman, according to McCall, "We haven't had much experience arresting sheriffs, but you can no longer identify the sheriff as being McCall in answering the phone or on any dispatch calls."

"That's when I first learned of it," McCall said.

State agents then showed up and arrested him in his office. "They said they were going to take me down and put me into court right away. I said, 'I'm not going.'

The chief circuit judge agreed to waive the defendant's appearance for a preliminary hearing, and McCall posted a bond of $1,000 at the courthouse and was allowed to remain free until his trial.

Governor Askew immediately suspended him from office.

"I am innocent," he said as he packed up a few things from his office into a cardboard box and left the building at midafternoon. He got into his gold-colored Oldsmobile and drove away. "I shall return."

Composite with sketch — This sketch of Sheriff Willis V. McCall is shown against a composite of headlines in Central Florida newspapers after the sheriff's indictment for second-degree murder and his suspension from office by Gov. Reubin Askew in June, 1972. (photo courtesy of Leesburg Commercial — Leesburg, Fla)

CHAPTER 30

IN LIMBO AFTER 28 YEARS

Gov. Askew's suspension took effect at 5 p.m. the same day the indictment was handed down. He cited "malfeasance, misfeasance, neglect of duty, incompetence or commission of a felony."

For the first time in 28 years, Willis McCall was out of office.

In a stinging public statement, Askew said McCall's treatment of Vickers showed "a depraved mind." He described the sheriff's actions as "willful inhumanity and oppression."

Maximum penalties upon conviction were thirty years imprisonment for second-degree murder and five years each for aggravated battery and aggravated assault.

In the stilted language of the law, the grand jury charged that Sheriff McCall "by an act eminently dangerous to another and evincing a depraved mind regardless of human life, although without any premeditated design to effect the death of any particular individual, (did) kill and murder Tommy J. Vickers in said Lake County by kicking him in the stomach and abdomen."

The indictment continued:

"Tommy J. Vickers, from April 13 until April 19, lay on the metal floor of the Creech Tank, in his own excrement and uneaten food, without a mattress or pad to sleep on. So far as the grand jury could determine, he was removed one time by Jailer (Clarence) Loudermilk for a bath, and again on the 19th of April when he was bathed and transferred to a hospital cell awaiting transport to the Waterman Memorial Hospital on April 20. . ."

The jury determined that McCall had petitioned the county court on April 14 for a mental examination of Vickers. "Nevertheless, from the date of his confinement . . . until the date of his death, Tommy J. Vickers was never presented before a judge or magistrate."

The indictment also charged McCall with threatening the jail prisoners scheduled to testify at the coroner's inquest following Vickers' death. The jury said McCall had each prisoner brought individually into his office "and gave them to understand and believe that they must testify according to the account stated to them by McCall. Each prisoner believed that unless he so testified he would be punished after being returned from court to the jail."

The reaction to the indictment in the county ranged from strong support of the sheriff to a cautious "wait-and-see" attitude.

"I think it's a frame-up," said Harvey Spears, a well-known general contractor.

Mayor Phil Conant of Umatilla said it was regrettable that the longtime sheriff 's actions have "again been brought under public question."

Leesburg Mayor Pyles saw it as "bad publicity for the county, where we have enjoyed good law and order."

"Maybe his sins have come home to rest," said another citizen who would not be identified. In the next breath, he said, "McCall is still boss of Lake County and you better not forget it."

The sheriff's longtime journalistic nemesis, Mabel Reese, said the indictment "has come twenty years too late."

Appointed acting sheriff to replace McCall was retired FBI agent Frank F. Meech, who had served as assistant to the mayor of Indianapolis before moving to Florida. His mother and father lived in Tavares for many years.

Meech kept all of McCall's deputies and office staff, a total that had grown to 33 people, including Deputy Malcolm McCall, the sheriff's son. Like Malcolm, most of the deputies and jailers had never worked for any sheriff other than McCall, and some had been born during his tenure.

Assigned to prosecute McCall was the same man who directed the grand jury investigation, the young, dapper Robert Eagan, anxious to make a name for himself as state attorney in Orange and Osceola counties. He was given broad authority by the governor to look into any other allegations of misconduct leveled against the sheriff.

Edgar Dunn, the governor's general counsel, said there were "lots of rumors of misconduct." He said his office had received telephone calls and letters complaining of some of McCall's activities in the past.

Uncharacteristically, McCall kept his silence. Reporters, who were already applying the "legendary" label to his name, couldn't find him at his newly built Lake Omega ranchhouse outside Umatilla. A new man sat at his office desk, and he made himself scarce.

McCall's supporters contended that the whole affair was politically motivated and that Circuit Judge Hall was deeply involved. Hall, who had a strong following in the county, was supposedly helping Askew, the young, politically ambitious governor, to curry favor with blacks and other Lake County groups.

McCall and Troy Hall had been boyhood friends, but their political views and ambitions led to petty feuds and serious conflict.

Hall was a big, burly man who had played football for Stetson College, just a few miles down the road in DeLand, in the 1930s. He had been an army officer in World War II and, as a reserve captain, had formed the Leesburg unit of the National Guard.

The sheriff claimed long and loudly that Hall had illegally

maneuvered the transfer of the grand jury investigation to Orange County along with Askew and Eagan.

"I could see that SOB Hall looking down on us from a window of the courthouse as Malcolm and I carried my stuff out to the car," McCall told me about the day he grudgingly left his office under suspension.

Their backbiting could be bitter, but oldtimers recalled humorous stories involving sheriff and judge.

One favorite story was born during the 1960 election, when then-County Judge Hall was running for the circuit court and McCall for reelection. According to the tale, the judge came upon an acquaintance wearing a campaign button that bore the legend: "Hall for Judge and McCall for Sheriff."

Hall stopped the man on the street and said, "John, you know how Willis and I feel about each other, how could you be for both of us?"

"Well, judge," came the reply, "I vote for Willis to protect me from the niggers and I vote for you to protect me from Willis."

Another oft-repeated story concerned a chance encounter between Hall, the sheriff and McCall's oldest son, Malcolm, at a civic function.

In front of a mutual friend, Hall praised young McCall. He said Malcolm proved the point that even an old SOB like Willis could have a fine son. The mutual friend was astonished by the remarks and expected fisticuffs. Instead, McCall smiled, gave his long cigar a contemplative twirl and replied, "It's too bad your father couldn't have been so lucky, judge."

Before his indictment, McCall had announced he would be running for an eighth term in that fall's elections. Now, few believed he would be convicted, and even fewer thought he could not win another four-year term of office after an acquittal.

Two days after the indictment, Florida Supreme Court Justice James C. Adkins Jr. was appointed to preside as judge at McCall's trial for second-degree murder. Chief Justice B.K. Roberts said there was "nothing new" about his assignment of a high court justice to a trial court.

Troy Hall and three other judges of the 5th Judicial Circuit had quickly excused themselves from the case.

Although not "new," the assignment of Adkins was highly unusual. It meant that the murder trial would be in the hands of officials with no connection to Lake County. It would probably be moved to another county out of that circuit. Officialdom seemed to be coming down hard on McCall.

Adkins was 57, a native of Gainesville and widely known as a scholar and author on criminal law, an ideal choice by the chief justice.

CHAPTER 31

MCCALL CAMPAIGNS, GOES TO COURT

On June 26, 1972, Willis McCall pleaded innocent to the three charges in circuit court in Tavares. He had celebrated his 63rd birthday the previous week.

He was subdued in court and wore a brown suit and a brown-and-blue checkered tie in place of his familiar black string tie and western-style clothes and boots. He solemnly shook hands with friends and looked around the courtroom as he sat down.

Judge Adkins set a trial date of August 15. As expected, Eagan asked that the trial be moved from Lake County because residents could be "fearful of bringing in a verdict" against the suspended sheriff. Adkins said he would rule on this later.

Earlier that June, a month after his murder indictment, McCall was the first in line as qualifying opened for the primary elections.

"I've done this eight times now. It's nothing new. I'm counting on winning," he said, reminding everyone that he had planned all along to run for an eighth consecutive term.

The time appeared to be ripe for a run against the old sheriff, however.

He drew three opponents for the Democratic nomination: Robert A. Locke Jr. of Leesburg, Robert D. Spears of Eustis and

Edward C. Hamrick of Leesburg. They were all former police officers. The only candidate filing for the Republican nomination was Guy Bliss, who had unsuccessfully opposed McCall as a Democrat in 1960.

Meech, the former FBI man who was acting sheriff, decided against running for election to the four-year term.

In due course, Judge Adkins decided to hear arguments on the prosecutor's motion for a change of venue. McCall's three lawyers argued strenuously against a move out of Lake County, contending that the Constitution called for a speedy public trial in the county where the crime was committed. The defense produced nine county residents who said they could render a fair and impartial verdict based solely on the evidence. The prosecution countered with eight others who said it would be difficult to seat an impartial jury.

One of the state's witnesses was a former deputy who alleged that McCall had a reputation for retribution and violence. Noel E. Griffin Jr. said he had been fired by McCall in 1961, ostensibly "for hog stealing." But he said the charge was trumped-up because he told the sheriff one of his deputies was taking money from moonshiners in adjacent Volusia County.

"There are only two kinds of people in Lake County: those who are against McCall and those who are for him," Griffin told the court in a strong voice. "There is no middle ground, no impartiality."

Gordon Savage, a former Leesburg mayor and Gov. Askew's patronage boss in the county, told the judge the trial should be moved because McCall "can charm a snake."

Adkins ruled that the trial be moved to Ocala.

The firm-jawed, bespectacled Adkins said the defendant himself had helped dictate the change of venue. He had waived his right to be tried in Lake County because of his election candidacy and the statements he had made on television preceding the grand jury investigation. The judge noted that the trial would be conducted during the height of the election campaign.

Ocala was a centrally situated venue and seemed to be a popular site for court people, prosecutors and judges. It was not a
big-city place like Jacksonville or Miami, and trials and hearings
could be conducted under more modest circumstances without a
lot of travel involved for the participants.

It was where Sheriff McCall had undergone scrutiny by a
federal grand jury during the Samuel Shepherd-Walter Irvin case.
The sheriff had not been indicted, and Irvin was later retried in
Ocala and again sentenced to die for the Groveland rape.

While all the pretrial legal maneuvering was going on, the
suspended sheriff's friends were busy building a defense fund.

Budge Meade, president of the first National Bank in Eustis, McCall's old citrus-industry friends C.V. Griffin and Charlie
Bradshaw, and other prominent business and professional people
were instrumental in the fund-raising effort for McCall's "fight
against his enemies."

They, along with Dr. C.M. Tyre, kicked in $1,000 each to get
started, and others quickly joined in, including Ted Mittendorf
of the St. Regis Paper Co. and Joe Creamons of the Oldsmobile-
Cadillac Dealership. A barbecue picnic in Mount Dora brought
in numerous donations, and there were many contributions from
around the state.

The fund grew to $35,000, enough so that McCall did not
have to spend a penny of his own money on the case.

Feelings ran high in Lake County. The campaign for the September 12 primary got under way and McCall and his opponents
began stumping in the small towns and rural settlements, drum-
ming up votes. Posters and bumper stickers reading "Keep Mc-
Call Sheriff" were as numerous as straw hats and pickup trucks.

Sentiments swayed, but one strongly voiced opinion was
that despite his notoriety, McCall had enforced "lawandorder"
throughout his long tenure. His supporters believed he would
once more prevail over the whole lot of them – governors, investigators, lawyers, judges, political turncoats.

Others argued that McCall had had his day. He had grown

old in the job and was fast becoming an anachronism in an area undergoing rapid change from a quiet, rural section of orange groves and cattle ranches to one of creeping urbanization and modern ideas from a growing population.

The county's population had evolved from about 28,500 when he was first elected to an estimated 75,000 in 1972.

Another disturbing note for the McCall camp: Several large campaign billboards depicting a smiling McCall in his white Stetson were chopped down and destroyed. One near Groveland was set afire.

While politics and interest in the coming trial held sway in Lake County, there was little attention given to such matters in the more-urbanized Ocala, which was also the center of Florida's horse-breeding industry.

The trial promised to be a classic courtroom confrontation between a young, ambitious urban prosecutor and an oldtime Southern lawman who inspired either fervent loyalty or bitter hatred, and hardly anything in-between.

Like the principal antagonists, the country courthouse was a study in contrasts between the old and the new. Inside, it was all steel and glass and futuristic design, but out on the lawn, a tall column supported a statue of a Southern infantryman leaning on a musket: a memorial to the Confederate dead.

A Smiling Sheriff — Lake County Sheriff Willis McCall shows up in court (right) with one of his three lawyers for a pretrial hearing in response to a second-degree murder indictment for the death of a black prisoner in his jail cell (photo courtesy of the Leesburg Commercial – Leesburg, Fla.)

CHAPTER 32

SHERIFF ON TRIAL

Suspended Sheriff Willis McCall, looking like a kindly, white-haired grandfather, appeared in court wearing a smart brown suit and black shoes. He didn't look the burly, tough-talking segregationist pictured in editorial cartoons and the columns of *Time Magazine, Ebony* and newspapers throughout the country.

He was accompanied by his wife, Doris, and smiled, waved and shook hands with spectators before sitting down at the defendant's table.

The judge had denied a last-minute attempt by the defense to keep the trial in Tavares. Jury selection began promptly at 9:30 a.m. on Tuesday, Aug 15, 1972.

McCall began cleaning his fingernails with a pocketknife. He didn't seem like a man facing a possible 30-year prison sentence for murder and an inglorious end to almost three decades of power as a lawman.

An all-day grilling of 82 prospects produced an all-white jury of four men and two women, plus a man and a woman as alternates for the second-degree murder trial.

Five blacks were called. Two were excused at their own request and three dismissed on peremptory challenges by head defense attorney Hubert Williams. One of those knocked off the jury was Maxcey Farmer, a farm laborer and distant cousin of James Farmer, a founder of the Congress for Racial Equality.

The defendant appeared to doze for a few minutes during jury-selection.

Those chosen to weigh the evidence were Bradley B. Bennett, Ocala clothing store manager and at 31 the youngest of the jurors; William R. Brown, operator of a convenience store; bank Clerk Mary Jane Braddock; real estate saleswoman Dee A. Walther; John H. Couse, a retired air conditioning salesman; and Frederick W. Bush Jr., also in real estate.

Interestingly (and deliberately on the part of the prosecution), none of them were native to the immediate area; three of them had moved to Marion County from other states.

In his opening statement the following day, Eagan told the jury that Vickers began creating a disturbance as soon as he was brought in from Miami and jailed in Tavares. The inmate kept yelling and pounding on the door throughout the night.

"The next morning, when Sheriff McCall came to work, the noise continued . . . Evidence will prove that Willis June and Jackie Huffman, both trusties, grabbed Vickers and pinned him down on the floor. Deputy Lucius Clay, jailer Jay Ramer and trusty Bobby Huffman were all there at the time," the prosecutor recounted methodically.

"Vickers resisted them and McCall said, 'That damn nigger ain't crazy.' "He then kicked Vickers three times with great force."

Pointing to the defendant and then turning to the jurors, Eagan said Sheriff McCall was wearing shoes at the time of the altercation with the prisoner, instead of his usual cowboy boots, but that "they were lethal weapons because of the manner they were used."

"Later in the afternoon, Vickers was put in a metal box designed for mental patients or used for punitive measures for unruly prisoners," the prosecutor continued. "Vickers stayed in this box for six or seven days with no toilet or even a hole (for bathroom use). When he came out he had lost weight and was in obvious physical distress.

"The jailer called a doctor, who recommended Vickers be taken to the hospital," the prosecutor continued. "Three days later, Tommy Vickers died of acute peritonitis caused by a blow to the abdomen."

Defense attorney James Robertson reserved his opening statement until after the prosecution rested its case.

One of the first prosecution witnesses, Acting Sheriff Meech testified that the transfer of a prisoner for a traffic offense was routine procedure when no bond was posted and he failed to return for trial. The sheriff can only follow his duty to serve a warrant issued by a judge, he said.

Brothers Jackie and Bobby Huffman, jail trusties and white, testified they entered Vickers' cell the morning of April 13 with another trusty, a black man named Willis June. Baby-faced Jackie Huffman, who had six felony convictions on his record, was serving a year in the Lake County jail for aggravated assault. His brother Bobby also had six convictions, including assault with intent to murder.

Jackie Huffman testified that when they opened the door to Vickers' cell, the inmate charged them and began hitting the sheriff. McCall told the trusties, Jackie Huffman and Willis June, to grab Vickers and as they did so, they tumbled to the floor with him.

"The sheriff kicked Vickers in the stomach three or four times, hard," Jackie Huffman testified. "Vickers tried to get up and we set him down again. He got to his hands and feet. The sheriff hit him behind the ear and he just lay there."

Jackie Huffman said he struck Vickers on the forehead, right between the eyes, with a "slapjack" when he was helping move the struggling inmate out of the holding cell into the creech tank.

Under cross examination, Jackie Huffman said he lied when he told the coroner's inquest that the sheriff only hit Vickers with a judo chop on the back of the neck. He never mentioned

McCall kicking the prisoner, Huffman testified, because he was afraid of McCall.

The defense contested this, arguing that Jackie Huffman was lying in court because he was afraid he and his brother might be charged with the murder of Vickers.

Bobby Huffman then testified he saw the sheriff kick the prisoner twice in the stomach, once in the kidneys and once between the shoulder blades.

Under defense questioning, Bobby admitted that he, too, had struck Vickers in the face, after the inmate hit him.

McCall's lawyers elicited testimony from both brothers that they expected to have their sentences reduced because they testified against McCall during the grand jury investigation. Jackie even revealed he had approached Judge Hall and asked him for a lighter sentence. He said Hall refused.

Former jailer Clarence Loudermilk told the jury Vickers was held in the creech tank six or seven days and fed a "punishment diet" of peas and carrots for several days until Loudermilk had it changed. He said he allowed Vickers to take showers twice, and that he cleaned the creech tank. When the inmate emerged from the tank, the jailer said, he was painfully thin; he appeared to have lost thirty or forty pounds.

McCall sat at the defense table, doodling on a yellow pad and working a crossword puzzle. But he did not doze off as he had the first day.

The defendant became a "witness" for the prosecution on the third day of the trial when Eagan introduced the suspended sheriff's testimony from the grand jury hearings in Orlando.

The prosecutor read from the transcript, and court reporter Frank Sarli read McCall's answers in a strong voice. The trial court heard McCall's version of what happened the morning of the violent incident with Vickers, as told to the grand jury.

McCall said he was probably wearing shoes since he rarely wore his boots during the summer months; that Vickers had become violent, thrown food at him and then wrestled on the floor with the two trusties. At that point, McCall said he put his foot on Vickers' arm and that he "flipped like a cat." It was then, McCall testified, that he struck the inmate on the back of the head.

The following day, according to the grand jury testimony, McCall signed an order to transfer Vickers to the mental health section of Waterman Hospital in Eustis. Because of "legalistic" delays, this was not done immediately, he said.

The defendant described the inmate as "strong as a mule." He said he found out later that Vickers was a mental case because "down in Dade County he was chopping up a cat with a hatchet and running around saying his brother was going to kill him."

Asked by Eagan at the grand jury hearing whether he met with any of the jailers and trusties after Vickers' death, McCall testified that he had and had told them to tell the truth, to "tell what is right."

The court reporter then read out what McCall told the grand jury:

"I wish you could have been in jail with a man like that. We don't need this kind in jail. There comes a time when you have to be firm, but I wouldn't hurt anyone. . . Some prisoners will tell anything to get days off their sentence."

McCall told the grand jury the investigation was politically motivated. And he named Judge Hall and Bill Reed, head of the Florida Department of Law Enforcement, as his political enemies. He said there was "bad blood" between him and Reed. "They (the agency) didn't give a damn about law enforcement. They haven't treated me right."

Asked by Eagan if he thought Gov. Reubin Askew was "out to get him," McCall replied, "Could be."

As to Vickers, McCall told the grand jury, "There is not a person here who wouldn't do what I did. I didn't violate his civil rights. I did nothing wrong."

The prosecutor then called two pathologists: Dr. Shutze, the district medical examiner for Lake and Marion counties; and Dr.

Thomas Hegert of Orlando, the Orange County medical examiner.

They both testified Vickers died due to peritonitis brought by "severe traumatic blow." Neither pathologist could say whether the peritonitis was definitely caused by a kick, but they told Eagan it seemed the most likely way it could have occurred.

Neither doctor could pinpoint the date of a blow that could have caused death. Shutze said it could have been from four-to-fourteen days. Hegert said from six-to-nine days.

Shutze performed his autopsy three days after the inmate's death. Hegert said he had the body exhumed on June 21 in Dublin, Georgia, where Vickers was buried.

Dr. Shutze also discovered scars from a skull fracture years earlier, presumably the result of a motorcycle accident suffered by Vickers at that time.

The prosecutor rested his case at the end of two days of testimony.

Hubert Williams immediately asked Judge Adkins for a directed verdict of acquittal, arguing the state had failed to prove anything except that a fatal blow or blows "could have been delivered April 13."

The defense lawyer argued that Eagan "did not prove that any particular wound caused death, or that McCall's shoes were a deadly weapon, or that great bodily harm was done to the subject."

After listening to Williams' and Eagan argue for several minutes, the judge interrupted and said, "You make a fine argument, Mr. Williams. But I'm going to deny your motion."

CHAPTER 33

McCall's Testimony

The defense went into action.

Williams' colleague, John Robertson, launched into his opening statement. He told the six-person jury that Tommy Vickers was a violent person who had been diagnosed in Miami as being paranoid-schizophrenic.

"The defense will show that Sheriff McCall is not the first police officer to have had trouble with Vickers," he said. "We will show there were three incidents in the Dade County jail at Miami, in one of which a police officer had to go to a hospital after he was injured by Vickers."

Robertson asserted that Vickers could have suffered the fatal injury in any of several fights in Miami or that the Huffman brothers could have caused the prisoner's death. The Huffmans beat Vickers on the night he was admitted and again early the next morning before the sheriff came in to the jail, Robertson said.

"We will have a number of prisoners testify and they will tell you that Vickers received a severe beating from the Huffmans on at least two other occasions. They bragged about this before the inquest, telling others about to testify to forget all they knew about the fight."

Larry Green, a jail inmate at the time, was brought to the stand and said he saw Vickers before McCall arrived and that he looked "as though he had been in a fight." Green said Jackie Huffman told him he beat Vickers. Huffman later bragged he had put Vickers to sleep with a blackjack, Green said.

Another inmate, James Kennington, testified he saw Jackie Huffman slug Vickers with a blackjack and that both Huffmans had told him they had beaten the black prisoner. He said they laughed, joked and bragged about it.

One jail inmate brought in the next day, a Friday, became a real challenge for defense lawyers. They had some shaky moments with Willis June, a tattooed, Afro-coiffed black jail trusty. He was considered a key witness to the violent jailhouse incident, but he had changed his story several times and Eagan finally gave up on him as a prosecution witness. The defense then hoped that June would support an earlier deposition saying he did not see McCall kick Vickers.

So June, a tall, rangy man, was brought on the stand as a "court witness," with the jury instructed as to why neither side would vouch for him.

When Williams hesitatingly asked him the all-important question, June nodded, glanced at McCall and replied:

"Yes, sir – I saw Sheriff McCall kick him in the stomach."

Members of the jury stirred, and there was nervous coughing in the audience.

Momentarily stunned by the unexpected answer, the defense lawyer then read portions of the deposition June had made to him earlier and asked the witness why he had changed his story.

"Must I tell you the reasons I told you these things?" June asked warily. "No," Williams shrugged and moved away. "I'll let Mr. Eagan ask you why."

The prosecutor was all too eager to ask, and June replied in cross-examination:

"I was scared when I told Mr. Williams that Sheriff McCall didn't kick Tommy Vickers. The sheriff's son drove me to Mr.

Williams' office and sat right there while I was talking. I'm a black man in Lake County. I was still in that jail at the time. I could have got myself killed."

Later, deputy Malcolm McCall testified that he had driven June to the defense lawyer's office but had stayed in an outer office while the interview took place.

The defense then introduced its ace-in-the-hole – a tape recording made when Willis June met with agents of the Florida Department of Law Enforcement in the back room of a Leesburg church. June had been transferred out of the jail in Tavares, and the clandestine meeting was arranged by Gordon Savage, the country patronage chief for Governor Askew and longtime political foe of Willis McCall.

All were Democrats, but party loyalty was not an issue in these feuds.

June was unaware that the meeting was being recorded by the FDLE agents. (At one point, June asked an agent what he was holding, and the agent replied that it was a dial-a-prayer machine).

The hushed courtroom heard June say on the audiotape recording that he did not see McCall kick Vickers and that he believed "the Huffmans killed him."

The tape ran for almost two hours. Although some of it was hard to understand, it strongly indicated that the agents were trying to prevail upon June to change his story for the grand jury investigation. June, however, repeatedly expressed fear that he would be found out if he told agents what they wanted to hear.

"Where's my protection," the deep, resonant voice of June asked at one point. "I'm a black man in Lake County."

A voice identified as that of Savage replied, "That's why I'm here."

He went on to tell June that he knew all about McCall.

"That man has been over there 28 years and we know that things have happened over there we have never been able to pin on him," Savage's recorded voice said. "Governor after governor has tried. . . . This is one time we can get him. . . . We are here as a direct result of the governor's action"

Savage tried to reassure June by saying, "There is a very good chance" the grand jury will not convene in Lake County. "Gov. Askew is well aware of Lake County justice."

June then started talking, explaining Vickers' beating in detail. "They beat him, really beat him."

But the inmate did not incriminate the sheriff.

The audiotape was revealing in that it supported McCall's claims that there were a number of officials out to get him politically. Savage was well known as the governor's man in Lake County. County residents also were aware that Savage and Judge Troy Hall were close allies against the sheriff.

Savage was called to the stand later and downplayed his role in the investigation. He told the jury that a former inmate has brought June to him for the meeting. He didn't say why they met in the back room of the Leesburg Methodist Church.

After that, there was testimony that the prisoner was kept in protective custody by the state, housed in various motels in several communities and given spending money. When agents discovered that June was staying drunk on state money and changing his story to fit the occasion, they dropped him from the list of prosecution witnesses.

In his deposition to defense lawyer Williams, June claimed the FDLE agents told him what to say and tried to get him to swear that McCall was wearing his cowboy boots when he entered Vickers' cell. He said, in return, the agents "guaranteed me they were going to drop my sentence."

The defense then brought in even heavier artillery. Two of the nation's leading pathologists cast doubts on Eagan's principal argument that Vickers' death was caused by kicks to the stomach.

The experts were Dr. Milton Helpern, chief medical examiner for the City of New York and the dean of the country's forensic pathologists; and Dr. William Sturner, medical examiner for Dallas County, Texas.

The silver-haired Helpern told the intent jury members he had personally performed 25,000 autopsies and assisted with 80,000 others. He refused to be pinned down by the lawyers as to the cause of the injury that caused Vickers' peritonitis. But he told the jury firmly:

"If that peritonitis had been caused by kicking, I would expect to find some bruising; if not on the abdomen itself, certainly on the soft tissues of the abdominal wall. The autopsy records show there was no such bruising. Therefore, I can only conclude that the peritonitis was caused by some other kind of blow."

Sturner, who said he had participated in 19,000 autopsies, agreed with Helpern. He went further by trying to establish the kind of blow that would not leave a bruised area.

"In the absence of bruising, I would have to say the injury was caused by a single, sharp blow – by a fist or the corner of a table, perhaps, not by kicks."

This fit in nicely with defense arguments that the Huffman brothers were lying when they claimed McCall kicked Vickers several times in the abdomen, and that the fatal injury probably was caused by jail trusties.

Helpern estimated the fatal blow could have come between six and fourteen days before death, but he also conceded that "It would be scientific guesswork to say how long before death it could have been delivered."

Sturner said the blow could have been within seven days and up to twenty days prior to death. The latter period would have put it back to April 3. Vickers was taken to Tavares on April 12.

The prosecutor noted the time frame also was within the period when the alleged jailhouse kicking took place. Eagan asked Helpern if a single kick could have caused the injury. Helpern said it could have but that he considered it unlikely.

Judge Adkins had informed the jury earlier in the week that they would be working on Saturday, when he expected them to receive the case from the lawyers and return a verdict. Suddenly the unusual Saturday session was at hand.

CHAPTER 34

McCall Testifies, Jury Delivers Verdict

The suspended sheriff, now a murder defendant fighting to stay out of prison, took the witness stand early on the final day for a little more than a half hour. He wore a blue suit, with an Elks Lodge pin on his coat and an elk tooth on his vest.

He tried a tight smile and then a glare before replying to the first question: "No," he had not kicked Vickers.

Looking directly at the attentive jurors, McCall testified that after hearing a loud noise on the morning he arrived at the county jail, he discovered the problem. Vickers was screaming and had thrown food out of his cell. The sheriff ordered the inmate to hand him the plate from the floor.

"You come and get it," was Vickers' reply.

"Sit down and behave yourself," McCall ordered from outside the cell.

"You come in here and make me," the prisoner yelled.

McCall said he unlocked the cell door and walked in.

"What happened then?" his lawyer asked.

"He charged me, and I backed up, not because I was afraid or anything like that, but I didn't want to get all messed up in that food on the floor. I had already slipped a little bit. I told the boys

170

(the two inmate trusties) to get ahold of him and sit him down on the bench."

They grabbed Vickers, and all three fell on the floor," McCall testified. "Vickers was choking one fellow, and I said in a scolding voice, 'Turn him loose.'"

One of the trusties took that to mean for Vickers to be turned loose, and the trusty broke his grip on the prisoner, McCall said. Then, gesturing:

"Vickers' arm was out there like that. I put my foot down on his arm and he flipped over. He was down there on his hands and knees, snortin' and a-snarlin' like a bull getting ready to charge. I popped him twice here on the back of the head (snapping his hands together and creating a loud popping sound). I told him to behave himself."

The trusties sat Vickers down on the bench and everyone left, he said. Later, the sheriff signed an order calling for incompetency proceedings against the prisoner. McCall went on vacation the following day.

Vickers was sent to the hospital seven days later.

In a brief, heated exchange, Eagan tried to break McCall's story.

The prosecutor accused McCall of trying to intimidate the witnesses. He said one of McCall's deputies, Lucius Clark, who saw the whole thing, "told you he wasn't going to lie for you this time, didn't he?"

"No!" came the angry reply.

Clark and jailer Jay Ramer testified earlier that they went with the sheriff to Vickers' cell but had then walked away down the hall and didn't go into the cell with McCall.

"Was Ramer guarding the area so no one could see what was going on?" Eagan asked.

"No!"

Judge Adkins then denied another defense motion for acquittal, and closing arguments began.

The prosecutor told the six jury members the case concerned

the rights and dignities of the individual, the trust in an officer of the law, and that officer's treatment of his fellow man.

"Vickers was not a criminal. He was only in the jail because he had been picked up for an invalid inspection sticker. Vickers isn't here; the only people who can testify are three felons and McCall. McCall has as much motive, or more, as the felons."

McCall was guilty of a "tragic betrayal of public trust," the prosecutor said."He has tried every way in the world to blame this on someone else, but he is the man in charge of the jail. Of the four persons who were in the cell at the time – felons though they may be – all testified Mr. McCall kicked Vickers, saying 'he ain't crazy, he ain't crazy.'"

Raising his voice but with little emotion, Eagan told the jury, "I feel it is your duty to find this man guilty of second de- gree murder."

Hubert Williams made the final argument for the defense, contradicting Eagan as to the issues of the case.

It was not a question of human rights and dignity of indi- viduals, the defense attorney said.

"It's not about Creech tanks, not about peas and carrots. . . You don't ask a jury to convict a man for murder because the prosecutor is convinced the jails need looking into."

Jurors had to consider only whether McCall caused Vickers' death, Williams said, as if lecturing.

The state "abused its power" in prosecuting McCall. The only thing in the world he can be convicted of is being sheriff and doing a job," he said. "McCall's political enemies don't like this old-fashioned person who still believes in right and wrong, still believes in morality."

He described the defendant as a man who said and did what he believed in because he was proud, honest and outspoken.

The state's star witnesses, the Huffman brothers, "lied and lied and lied," Williams argued, adding that two of the country's leading pathologists testified the fatal blow was not a kick to the stomach.

"If there is a larger issue in this case, it is whether a lawman has a right to keep order in his own jail."

With that, the judge turned the case over to the jury at almost 5 o'clock Saturday afternoon.

Deputies and bailiffs mingled with the spectators as the judge and jury retired. Williams had earlier reported receiving two threatening telephone calls, and this resulted in a sudden security crackdown. Everyone had been frisked, including jurors and reporters. No weapon was found.

Outside, it was raining, and Shriners congregated from all over the state were getting wet on the downtown streets of Ocala during their annual parade.

One hour and fifteen minutes later, the four men and two women filed back into the jury box. The judge formally asked if they had reached a verdict.

Brad Emmett, the foreman, stood and said, "Yes, we have, your honor."

Judge Adkins, the Florida Supreme Court justice sent to preside over a controversial murder trial because of the political turmoil, looked quickly at the jury note and told Court Clerk John Nicholson in a booming voice, "Publish the verdict, Mr. Clerk."

Nicholson read: "Not guilty." Not guilty." "Not guilty."

Acquittal on all charges.

Doris McCall broke into sobs. Her husband looked around, went over and enveloped her in a bear hug.

Except for a loud gasp from some of the spectators, there were no outbursts, which the judge had sternly warned about. He thanked the jury, the lawyers, the press and walked out of the courtroom.

The principals were spirited out through a side door before the spectators were allowed to leave. McCall walked out with an arm around his wife. He shook hands with several people. His son, deputy Malcolm McCall, the sheriff of Marion County and some of McCall's friends followed them out the door.

On the side of the courtroom where most of the whites sat,

folks were smiling and crying and laughing. Most of those on the other side, which included some whites, were quiet, some saddened and sullen. There were no press interviews.

It had stopped raining.

Suddenly it was over for the "Big Hat Man," as Lake County blacks called him behind his back. He was free, again, of charges that he had done wrong. And he was on his way home.

Now for the election.

And, surely, Gov. Askew would lift the suspension and allow him to return to the office from which he had been temporarily removed. Things would be the same as before, and he would go on to an eighth-straight term. He had once again defeated his enemies and detractors.

He would once again be The Sheriff, the top *lawandorder* man in Lake County.

CHAPTER 35

POLITICAL TURMOIL, ERA ENDS

McCall's enthusiasm over his victory was dampened that Saturday evening when a spokesman for the governor announced in Tallahassee that Askew would continue McCall's suspension pending a State Senate hearing on allegations of malfeasance and misfeasance in office.

"Evidence in a suspension action is different from that in court," said Askew spokesman Don Pride.

The governor was clearly trying to derail McCall's plans to return to office. The Florida Legislature was not in session. A Senate hearing appeared unlikely at least until its organizational meeting after the November general election. If no emergency action was taken, the issue wouldn't be considered until after the legislative session began in April.

Of course if McCall won reelection in November, that would put pressure on Askew to lift the suspension by January, when elected officials were sworn in. There might not be need for the Senate to debate the merits of the governor's action and decide whether to remove McCall permanently or return him to office.

An election victory was not a guarantee of anything, however, and McCall knew it.

But he was determined, more than ever, to continue as sheriff of Lake County. And the young governor would have a fight on his hands to keep him out of the office he had held for 28 years.

There had been jubilation over the acquittal among the staff members in the sheriff's office. One deputy, Elbert Foster, told a reporter: "The interesting thing about this is that the old man wouldn't have run for reelection this time if this thing hadn't come up. He was going to retire."

Asked about this as he received friends and well-wishers at home on Sunday, McCall said, "Well, I was a lot closer to retiring than anybody thought I was. But then all this came up — and I wasn't going to retire in the face of all this."

He never lost confidence. "I knew I wasn't guilty. The newspapers tried me, and Eagan is their fair-haired boy. But the people know the truth."

As his own campaign manager, he planned to devote most of his time to getting elected again.

"I just go everywhere, see everybody. I just get out and campaign — meet and see people, just the regular routine." The trial would make no difference, he told me. "The people know me, know who I am . . . You want to lay odds on it?"

On Monday, the jury foreman, Brad Emmett, said the panel members took only one vote to arrive at their unanimous verdict of acquittal on all the charges. "There was no debate."

The contradictions posed in the testimony of the Huffman brothers made the difference, Emmett said. The jury didn't believe them, and the state didn't have a case without them.

Instead of simplifying matters, the McCall trial resulted in more turmoil — among Democrats, McCall supporters, his detractors and those only temporarily interested.

Askew would not let McCall off the hook despite calls by a number of legislators and a petition drive calling for him to be reinstated. Instead, the governor announced that the U.S. Justice Department was looking into the possibility of civil rights violations in the Vickers case. McCall could be prosecuted in federal court.

A governor's aide said the FDLE also was checking into reports that McCall carried a concealed weapon into court during his trial.

McCall himself had told reporters about it while waiting for the jury verdict on Saturday. He had a small pistol in his right pants pocket on the opening day of the trial. When his defense lawyers learned of it, they had him turn it over to a deputy acting as a bodyguard. McCall said he had been a lawman for so many years that carrying a pistol was as natural as putting his wallet and keys in his pockets as he dressed every morning.

Askew's office also announced that special prosecutor Eagan would continue looking into other aspects of McCall's actions as sheriff. The governor's general counsel, Edgar Dunn, said the sheriff's suspension had not been based entirely on the charges involving Vickers' death. There were "complaints involving conditions at the jail," for instance.

In addition to a petition calling for McCall's reinstatement, there was another asking for an investigation of Gordon Savage, the governor's political manager in Lake County.

The defense had disclosed that the former Leesburg mayor was instrumental in the grand jury probe leading to McCall's indictment, and it alleged that Savage had encouraged witnesses to commit perjury. Savage said he welcomed an investigation and had nothing to hide.

The petition calling for McCall's reinstatement, bearing thousands of signatures, went to State Senate President Jerry Thomas.

In another development, four of the prisoners taken to the Ocala Jail from Lake County to testify were released outright from custody. They included Jackie and Bobby Huffman, both of whom were serving one-year terms for aggravated assault.

State Attorney Don Nichols of Jacksonville was appointed to investigate the allegations that the suspended sheriff had carried a weapon into the courtroom during his murder trial. Under the law, investigators had to come up with eyewitnesses.

Nichols and two investigators had rough going. Not one deputy in Ocala saw McCall armed. The judge didn't see it. Other court officers said they never saw McCall toting a weapon. There had been rumors but until he admitted it, none one had been sure.

Sparing Eagan from another embarrassing chore, Nichols also was assigned to investigate the complaint against Savage, the governor's man.

Gov. Askew's aides were soon saying that because of the new investigations, the suspended sheriff would *certainly not* be reinstated, no matter what happened in the upcoming elections.

It was like a comedy for awhile.

Back to real life: "I'm going to go ahead and get elected," McCall said confidently. "The people of Lake County understand the situation."

Florida's election code requires a runoff if the leading candidate in the primary election doesn't receive a clear-cut majority of the total vote. McCall had three opponents for the Democratic primary. On the Republican side, Guy Bliss faced no opposition, so he would be the GOP candidate for sheriff in November.

McCall sweated a bit on election day, but he pulled out a victory again. It was so close, however, that he had to wait until the 201 absentee ballots were counted to see about a clear majority. It was his tightest primary race.

Now, only Bliss blocked his path to another four-year term — plus a legal confrontation with the governor and legislature after that.

The man who hoped to end McCall's career as sheriff after seven terms was a tall, well-spoken former Detroit detective who looked more like a judge than a cop. Bliss spoke out against the two factors he said dominated McCall's long tenure: inefficiency and racism.

"McCall is an American Gothic original. The South has gotten rid of Bull Connor and Jim Clark, but McCall still rules Lake County. I think it's time we got rid of this 17th Century character and brought this county into the 20th Century where law enforcement is concerned."

Bliss was 57. He had retired to the area and entered politics, becoming a city councilman and mayor of Mount Dora and then a municipal court judge. Twelve years earlier, he had run against McCall in the Democratic primary and lost. Now, he had switched to the Republican side and was confident of beating the crusty sheriff, who all of a sudden appeared vulnerable.

"I'm running," Bliss told an interviewer, "because I know police work doesn't have to be done the way Willis McCall has been doing it."

Republicanism was on the rise, and the old sheriff's constituency was changing along with the times. Condos and mobile homes were beginning to replace citrus groves. New residents and new business interests meant new attitudes. The new people had no reason to hark back to the earlier days. They had few hidebound loyalties.

Bliss campaigned hard. He ridiculed McCall's claims that Communists and black militants were out to get him.

"He's been building that myth for 28 years at the taxpayers' expense. He even believes it himself by now," Bliss would say. "Here is a man who insults blacks, Jews, Catholics and runs for public office. He's the Archie Bunker of Lake County politics."

McCall insisted on depicting himself as the target of a host of enemies, including blacks, Commies and "ultraliberals."

To anyone who doubted it, he would show them scrapbooks filled with letters, telegrams, cards and other messages threatening him for one reason or another. One by the National Negro Congress said he had been "tried in absentia and condemned to death for your crimes against the Negro race." It was written on the letterhead of that organization and dated August 27, 1959.

But McCall refused to criticize Bliss.

"I prefer to run on my merits, not the other guy's demerits. . . He appears to be a decent fella."

Bliss, the Democrat turned Republican, was realistic. "Willis

McCall has done some bad things and some good things. I just think he's been doing them too long."

The inevitable happened.

It all ended for McCall on November 7, 1972. He lost the office he had held for 28 years by 2,178 votes. For once, he was speechless. He refused comment.

"Lake County is changing," Bliss said. "New people, new ideas, new business interests."

Perhaps the most-relieved person in the state was Gov. Askew. He might have had hard going in sustaining McCall's suspension in the Senate early the following year because of McCall's many devoted, and emotional, followers. The suspension remained in effect until the new sheriff took office, however.

An era ended with McCall's defeat at the polls. He had been stripped naked of more than a badge. He had devoted himself totally to his job as he saw it. "They" had finally succeeded in bringing him down. But it was through the ballot box, not through any investigations or legalities of grand juries and courtrooms.

He was the last of the strongarm enforcers of the Old South — the hard-line, staunchly conservative sheriffs who interpreted the law in their own fashion and ruled with an iron fist while affecting a just-folks, homespun manner.

There were no postmortems.

CHAPTER 36

AFTERMATH

More than 20 years went by in forced retirement. Willis V. Mc-Call had grown gray, somewhat mellow, but no less outspoken. He was still an imposing — though hardly an intimidating — figure in and around Lake County.

His life, and that of his neighbors, was much quieter now than in the three decades following his first election as sheriff, when his *lawandorder* exploits created headlines around the nation and brought notoriety to this sleepy, rural region where he was born.

Deep into the traditions of the Old South, Lake County thrived on citrus and a simpler life in those days. Now, in more modern times, the region had radically changed, not always for the good. Despite its booming population growth, much like the rest of Florida, it retained vestiges of the old days when life was slower and less complicated.

The citrus industry had declined in much of the state's mid-section, given way to frosty weather, condos and other development. But its small towns were livelier, a bit more spruced up, some busting at the seams.

In present terms, most folks — black, brown and white — are now generally considerate of each other, mainly law-abiding and churchgoing and many are still practicing the values stressed by their rural roots and small-town environments. There are many newcomers, of course, who don't know or don't care about Lake County's rich history or about one of the most-notorious lawmen to come out of the South.

Towards the end of a long, adventure-filled life, McCall's macho, pugnacious personality had been toned down, but he still had the vitality of a younger man. And he was still proudly recounting the old days, especially the 28 years when he ruled the county as sheriff.

He told me over and over that if he had a chance to do it again, he would do things in pretty much the same way.

"I did things the way I knew best, and I make no apologies for that," he said, sitting in the living room of his sprawling house at his Lake Omega ranch.

"We worked within the law, and that's the way things were. If you had to cuff somebody around 'cause he was violatin' and resistin' the law, you did it. That's the way things were done."

But, "I never seriously hurt anyone . . . or killed anyone that didn't deserve killing."

Up to the end, McCall kept his white hair cropped short, carefully combed and parted, still dressed in Western-styled shirts and suits, black string ties and ranch boots. His round face and glasses, his paunch and slow, easy manner gave him the appearance of an amiable grandfather.

McCall's grandparents homesteaded across this same lake near Umatilla shortly after the Civil War. He was born at their home. Now, he owned 300 acres, given over to pastureland and some citrus. For a long time, he kept a Palomino named Pretty Boy, a herd of goats, two hunting dogs and a couple of cats.

An occasional alligator slithered in from swampy canals, trying to make a meal of a baby goat. He'd been known to shoot them now and again (and was reprimanded by game officials). The alligator has long been a protected species in Florida. When a local newspaper once headlined a story, SHERIFF MURDERS

FLORIDA NATIVE, the ruckus it raised didn't die down until McCall had the animal eviscerated: The remains of a small dog were found in its stomach.

McCall chuckled over that many years later.

"They used to blame me for everything after I shot those niggers (Shepherd and Irvin) and spoke out against integration and things like that," McCall said good-naturedly. "They blamed me for everything but being a child of God . . . and taking a bath."

McCall always had a wry sense of humor, even when vilifying his critics, and he retained that characteristic to the end. He recalled the smallest details about his career. He used to sip iced tea and relax in an easy chair in his living room, with a view of Lake Omega, and to spread out on the coffee table large scrapbooks that Doris kept over the years.

The walls of a study were covered with plaques, certificates, photos. There was a photograph of George Wallace, who autographed it when he stopped in Lake County during his try for the Democratic presidential nomination in 1972. McCall even kept two signs a court had ordered removed from his front office in the 1970s. They read: "Black Waiting Room" and "White Waiting Room."

At one time, he owned some "nigger rental property" in Tavares, he said.

In a surprisingly soft, low voice that would hold a visitor's full attention, he would carefully go into the background of each frayed clipping, each photograph, each leaflet, the glued-on letters and brown, thinning Western Union telegrams. Some contained death threats, others praised him.

The news clips told of his murder trial, labor organizers, Communists, the South's integration battles and McCall's humanitarian work with the Elks Club and a crippled-children's hospital, which he helped to found and still oversaw like a mother hen. The tearsheets chronicled much of his public life, mostly in overbroad, platitudinous phrases.

He and Doris McCall kept it all — unlikely treasures.

"It's all in there. I can't deny the record. I'm not afraid of the truth," he emphasized to me. "I always spoke my mind, never made any secret of my feelings."

Reporters had a field day with this rambunctious lawman. Some made their reputations writing about his exploits. There was often good, hard-news reporting by on-the-scene correspondents, and there were many purple-prose features and "I-was-there" stories by outsiders who would sweep into Lake County after every major incident and become instant experts on the big, bad racist sheriff.

As it often does, the reporting made the legend.

"Trouble was," McCall said in defense, "Everybody wanted the controversy regardless of what the real facts were."

His friends, neighbors and those who voted him into office time-after-time saw him differently. Even some of those who didn't agree with his methods respected him as a strict law and order sheriff. And, significantly, he understood the way they thought, and what they wanted. From the local merchant to the lowliest packinghouse worker, from the wealthy grower to the black laborer who picked the fruit in the groves, from the auto mechanic to the shopgirl and poor dirt farmer — he understood them all. He was out among them every day.

McCall truly liked people, liked to talk, joke and deal with them on every possible occasion. He aggressively pursued the adventures of life and his job.

Much of his recklessness was the result of immediate reaction to circumstance, rather than calm, precise action. When he took the whip hand against those who had violated his standards of *lawandorder,* he could be mean and unyielding. There was little room for differing opinion or compromise.

There was no question or right or wrong: He was right.

But the stereotype of the Dumb Good Ol' Boy who used his power to excess — until they got rid of him — ignores his political acumen, his personal popularity, the support he received from so many devoted followers every step of the way.

The late Emmett Peter, a native of Leesburg and veteran reporter and editor in Lake County who frequently clashed with McCall both privately and publicly, told me, "I always thought he was a good law enforcement officer. He was suspicious of everybody. He knew how to ask questions and he never let go. He was a good country sheriff."

Professor Charles M. Uncovic of the University of Central Florida, who made a study of Southern sheriffs, explained McCall's popularity and power as coming from "a regular public accountability through the ballot box."

People kept electing him to office, and he translated the mandates as public acceptance of his policies.

Even in retirement McCall could cause a stir, however unwillingly.

At his urging, and that of friends and supporters, the Lake County Commission voted in 1985 to rename a three-mile section of County Road C-450. Commissioners unanimously decreed that the new name would be "Willis V. McCall Road." It ran right in front of his ranch. Commission members argued that the family had been there since the turn of the century and should be honored in this way.

McCall had circulated a petition to that effect among his ranching neighbors, and most had signed it. Acting after many belated protests, however, the commission rescinded its action in 2007 and renamed the road C450A.

Ormund Powers, a former correspondent and political writer in Lake County for the *Orlando Sentinel,* told me, "I thought he did a damn fine job of keeping law and order" (everyone who talks about McCall uses those words).

"Of course, McCall hated black people and that affected his judgment," Powers said. "On the whole, though, he had the support of the large majority of people in the county. They needed somebody strong in there. That's why they kept him so long."

Although McCall regretted little, he would have liked to

tweak his political enemies a little. At the top of the list would have been Gov. Reubin Askew and Judge Troy Hall, I'm sure.

But he did manage, in a roundabout way to even the score with the only man to defeat him in an election, Guy Bliss, the Republican who prevented him from getting elected to an eighth four-year term as sheriff.

When Sheriff Bliss came up for reelection in 1976, McCall and his son Malcolm saw a chance to even the score.

Malcolm was a respected criminal investigator in the office of the state attorney and had served more than 20 years as a deputy under his father. When election time came around in 1976, he decided to challenge Bliss. Willis McCall campaigned vigorously for his son, calling on old friends and his politically and financially influential supporters around the county.

Whether it was the McCall name, disillusionment over Bliss, good campaigning — or a combination of those things, plus a reawakening of stubborn, oldtime beliefs — the electorate responded. The 44-year-old Malcolm McCall defeated the man who had turned his father out of office four years earlier.

The younger McCall built a creditable record, streamlining the office, putting more deputies out in the field and staying within his budgets. But he wasn't the devil-be-damned kind of sheriff his father was, and he lost an attempt for reelection.

One of the last times I saw Willis McCall was in the kitchen of his ranchhouse. He and Doris, a small, quiet-spoken woman, persuaded me to join them for a late lunch. The big, bad ex-sheriff cut up and fried ham slices while his wife served macaroni and cheese, green beans from their garden, iced tea and homemade pound cake.

At my urging, Doris McCall reminisced a bit about the old days, expressing the hope that some day the good things her husband did would be as readily recognized as "those wild times they always wrote about."

Remembering their 50th wedding anniversary celebration some years before, Doris said someone jokingly asked her if she had ever thought of divorce in all that time. Now – eyeing her husband mischievously — she told me she had replied to her friend, "No, I never did. But I thought of shooting him once or twice."

McCall laughed uproariously at that.

He was 84 when he died in April, 1994.

A Reflective McCall – Former Sheriff Willis V. McCall of Lake County talks about his tumultuous 28 years in office and says he has few regrets about his actions: "I never hurt anyone . . . or killed anyone who didn't deserve killing." (photo courtesy of the Daily Commercial – Leesburg, Fla.)

AFTERWORD

There's little disagreement that Sheriff Willis Virgil McCall was a bigger-than-life character. He can be judged by his deeds.

He was a racist, a man who wielded power in the wrong way for far too long. He killed a prisoner in his custody and was put on trial for murder in the death of another convict in his jail cell.

He was mocked and parodied and brought ridicule to the very small part of the world he literally ruled with an iron hand for three decades. As most political animals, however, he was a walking paradox.

His almost three decades in office made for a hell of a ride, for McCall himself, the people of Lake County, and, in the end, for the whole world of law enforcement leading up to and through the United States Supreme Court.

About his denunciation by the Soviet Ambassador to the United Nations, Andrei Vishinsky, McCall would say he was just being a Communist! What d'ya expect?

During his lengthy tenure, Sheriff McCall's hellbent course in pursuing his own brand of *lawandorder* was the core of his being. But, as I say, he was a different man in private.

I have limited this account to events that might be considered the most interesting, or you might say outrageous.

Through much of his time, as we have seen, Sheriff McCall was the target of investigations by county, state and federal officials and grand juries, all hoping to find reason to punish him or throw him out of office. These investigations were carried out often — not once or twice, as may occur with some overly aggressive police people — but numerous times. He was always walking that thin line.

The thing of it is he kept getting elected to office. For 28 years, he seemingly represented the values of his constituents, or at least the voters, who gave him big electoral majorities. He was one of them in the truest sense. Consequently, the spotlight fell on him.

In his retirement, we spent many hours together — Saturday mornings, Sunday afternoons — for more than a year. He filled my head with his ideas of *lawandorder*. I filled notebooks. He opened up his personal files and official records.

Much of this time and effort was in trying to give me his side of the story. He simply wanted his reputation to outlive him and, if possible, to become even *bigger* than life. He would have liked for a movie to be made out of the book. He could see himself portrayed on the screen much like Brian Dennehy as Southern lawman Buford Pusser in "A Real American."

As a longtime journalist, however, I made him understand at the outset that I was the sole arbiter of everything I would write, that a manuscript would set down all the bad along with the good. I constantly reminded him that I would weigh what he said with the words of others, with court records, documents, letters and photographs.

He readily agreed to all of this all along the way, declaiming that he just wanted *his* side of the story to be presented along with what had been written and thrashed-about in reportage that resounded across the nation and even parts of Europe.

I've tried to be as objective as I can.

As you can see, there was much more to the man than the headlines. No one is truly all bad, of course, just as no one is truly all good. McCall had a soft-hearted side to him that few people saw.

For many years, he was one of the benefactors of the Boys Ranch at Umatilla, sponsored by the Florida Sheriffs Association. It helped troubled kids, steering many away from criminal lives.

McCall was outgoing and friendly with everyone who stood on his side of *lawandorder*. He was a family man, a joke teller, a deer hunter and, in later years, he liked getting together with friends and telling tall stories over a late breakfast at the Mason Jar restaurant of a Saturday morning. He was a nondrinker and a faithful churchgoer on Sundays.

You may, then, possibly ask why write all this down now after all these years? Who cares?

The answer — bear with me here — is that publishers in the 1970s and 1980s considered that the period of "The Big, Bad Southern Sheriff" was over, a subject that was no longer selling books. My manuscript was "thorough and convincing," said the editor-in-chief at Harcourt Brace Jovanovich, "a well-written book."

But controversial figures like McCall, he went on to say, are anachronistic and no longer commercially viable.

The publisher of MacMillan Publishing Co. called it "an interesting story — not unlike *To Kill a Mockingbird*." That was high praise. But she wouldn't publish it.

There were other publishers, editors and literary agents all saying the era was *passé*.

I grudgingly accepted that then. But over the years, I came to strongly disagree with that argument because McCall's story is really a part of history. *He* is a part of history.

To some extent, the remnants of that society still exist. But I'll leave that argument for historians, politicians and others.

This is true-to-life *nonfiction*. Truth really *is* stranger. A novelized characterization wouldn't do justice to the actual events, actions and direct quotes from McCall and all of those involved. This book is written in flowing, narrative form — no footnotes, bibliographies and such. Everyone who contributed, directly or indirectly, is cited within its pages.

I believe it is a good story in its own right. It is based on my own research and interviews. Only a few of the names have been changed for their protection.

Lake County is still a thriving little region in Walt Disney World's back yard, but its life in those days was s-o-o-o different.